Cooking with Fruits and Nuts

COOKING
WITH
FRUITS
AND
NUTS

Moira Hodgson

The Bobbs-Merrill Company, Inc.

INDIANAPOLIS AND NEW YORK

The Bobbs-Merrill Company, Inc.
INDIANAPOLIS • NEW YORK

FIRST PRINTING

for Philippa

Contents

Introduction

Now that the cooking of the Near and Far East, Latin America, the Mediterranean, and India has come to play an increasingly important role in our own, so fruits and nuts have come into greater use than before. Thanks to refrigeration and air transport, fruits from tropical countries and the Mediterranean, as well as hothouse fruits, are available to us.

In the Middle East the ancient rulers of Persia, Egypt, Greece, and Byzantium had a highly developed and sophisticated cuisine in which fruits and nuts played a large part. Fruits were added to main dishes, cooked as a vegetable, or used with nuts as a seasoning and an embellishment. Even today the Egyptians use ground almonds or pine nuts to thicken a sauce, as do the Persians. The Turks use ground walnuts, and the Persians add pomegranate or sour cherries to a walnut sauce. The Moroccans are particularly skillful in combining the textures of fruits and meat.

In India fruits and nuts, with their valuable protein and vitamins, replace meat for the vegetarian Hindu. In areas in which candy and dentists are unknown, people exist with perfect teeth, getting their sugar in a natural form and using nuts to clean their teeth after eating. Most Indian recipes, particularly curries, contain some combination of meat or vegetables with fruits or nuts.

In Latin America, where a marriage of Spanish and Indian cooking has taken place, the Indian tradition of using fruits and nuts has remained. Every Latin American regional cuisine features an abundance of fruit, such as pineapples, bananas, plantains, papayas, and mangoes (to name a few), which abound in the region. Sauces are thickened with ground almonds or pumpkin seeds. Fruits and nuts provide nutrition when meat or eggs are not available, and many of the poor subsist on little else during the season.

In Europe the apple is the fruit most often cooked with meat. German, Scandinavian, British, and Russian dishes use the apple extensively as a stuffing, a vegetable, or a garnish with strongly flavored meat. Cherries are also used in Russian and French cooking, as are grapes. The chestnut is used as both a vegetable and a sweet, and almonds are used in sauces for fish and chicken.

Not only can fruits and nuts be used as a basis for dishes, they can also be used to embellish and decorate dishes that might otherwise be bland or dull. The list is endless: sauces, stuffings, spreads, cakes, desserts, breads, stews, soups, pies are all easily enhanced by adding fruits and nuts. The look of food is very important, quite apart from its taste, and the bright colors of fruit or a sprinkling of nuts looks very well with main dishes. By adding a small embellishment here and there you can transform an ordinary meal.

Cooking with Fruits and Nuts

About Fruits

As most people know, fruit contains a large amount of vitamin C. It is also a natural source of sugar in its purest and most digestible form. It contains mineral salts essential to the body, and according to P. E. Norris, author of *About Fruits, Vegetables and Salads,* leaves an alkaline ash in the blood that maintains its balance and helps to keep you fit. He suggests that a human diet should consist of 80 per cent alkaline ash foods, and of the list he gives, fruit predominates.

Many of the vitamins and minerals are in the skin of the fruit. To get the most out of a piece of fruit, as far as nutrition is concerned, it should be very fresh, washed quickly, and eaten fairly soon. Unfortunately, spraying is now so universal that unless you buy organically grown fruit, you have to wash the peel very thoroughly (some say only hot water and soap will get all the sprays and fixing agents off), and in some cases it might be safer to remove it altogether.

Buy fruit in season when it is at its cheapest and freshest. It does not keep well and should be refrigerated; it should be stored for only a few days. Damaged fruits should be discarded; they can impart their bruises to the other fruit. Do not wash berries or cherries until just before eating them. Bananas should not be kept in the refrigerator; they will turn black.

Unripe fruit can be left to ripen at room temperature, away from direct sunlight.

Freezing robs fruit of its texture. When fresh fruit is in season, it is cheaper than frozen fruit. If you buy frozen fruit, make sure the package is hard, clean, and frost-free and that the store has a fairly constant turnover of frozen goods.

Canned fruit, like meat, is graded. The grades are:

Grade A or U.S. Fancy
Grade B or U.S. Choice
Grade C or U.S. Standard

These grades are based on the color, flavor, texture, shape, and freedom from defects in the fruit, according to a U.S. Department of Agriculture report. The higher grades look more attractive, but their nutritive value is the same as that of the lower ones.

Apples

The first apples may have grown in the Mediterranean area, parts of southeastern Europe, and southwestern Asia. They came to America with the early pioneers. They are a hardy fruit, able to survive severe cold and hot climates, provided there is a cool period during winter. Many varieties are available in the United States, including McIntosh, Granny Smith, Baldwin, Winesap, Yellow Newstone, and Golden Delicious. When you buy them, choose firm, unbruised apples and avoid those that feel spongy when you press them. Wash them very thoroughly since they are coated with poisonous sprays that have been sealed against the rain by fixing agents.

Apples are one of the most healthful of all fruits. They contain vitamins B and C, potassium, iron, and magnesium. They strengthen the blood stream, aid digestion, and help prevent kidney stones. They also help prevent tooth decay.

Apples are a versatile fruit and can be cooked as a savory or sweet dish. They may be served with pork, chicken, or ham, as stuffings or garnishes for game, as a vegetable, or in salads. They can also be cooked in various simple and inexpensive ways for dessert.

Crab apples are a small and more acid variety of apple. They are primarily used for pickles, jams and jellies, and cider and as garnishes for savory dishes.

Apricots

Apricots were known in China 3,000 years ago and in the United States in the early seventeenth century. They are now grown in France, Algeria, Spain, and the United States. Ripe, fully matured apricots are hard to find in the market today. Since they travel badly, they are picked when hard.

Elizabeth David, in *French Provincial Cooking*, describes the apricot as follows: "The beautiful, aromatically scented little golden fruit is the one with which I bracket the fig as being the most elusive and rare to find in perfect condition." Since we have no chance to "pocket the perfect ripe apricot warm from the sun," we are better off cooking the ones we can buy. A simple dessert of poached apricots can be delicious.

Dried apricots are very good with lamb, chicken, and other meat dishes.

Bananas

About 30 different species are known of the banana tree, which grows in tropical regions. It is one of the oldest fruits, mentioned in Sanskrit and ancient Chinese writings, and is believed native to Southeast Asia. In 1516 it was introduced to the New World. It is now imported to the United States from Central and South America.

Bananas are easy to grow and easy to transport. They can be picked and sold unripe and will ripen successfully at room temperature. They are also one of the most nutritious fruits, rich in minerals and easy to digest.

Plantains are a larger, firmer variety of banana, and they can only be eaten cooked. They are used as a vegetable and can be eaten fried, boiled, or baked. If you intend to cook ordinary bananas, slightly unripe ones will hold their shape better. Bananas, in addition to being used as a vegetable (page 54), can be cooked with fish, meat, or chicken or used as hors d'oeuvres or stuffings. When you buy them, choose firm green or yellow unspotted ones.

Blackberries

Blackberries are the fruit of the bramble bush, which belongs to the rose family. The bush is native to Asia, North America, and Europe. It grows wild along hedgerows, and when it is ripe, you can go out with a basket and collect the berries, which grow in abundance, protected by thorns and branches. There are hundreds of species of the berry. Loganberries are a cross between a blackberry and a raspberry. Both boysenberries and dewberries are varieties of the blackberry.

They are superb when freshly picked and eaten with a little sugar and fresh cream. They are also made into jams, jellies, wines, and cordials.

To prepare them, pick them over carefully and remove any hulls or stalks. Discard any moldy berries. Wash just before using by putting in a colander and running cold water over them. Drain well. Do not leave them sitting in water or pile them up and leave them overnight in the refrigerator. Spread them out on a large flat dish and sprinkle them with sugar. Keep cool until ready to eat.

Blueberries

Blueberries grow wild all over the United States and Europe and have only recently been cultivated. Unfortunately, someone must be running a contest to see who can raise the first blueberry the size of a golf ball. Every year they get larger and, sadly, more tasteless.

To prepare them, treat as for blackberries but wash them *very* thoroughly, as they have been treated with every conceivable chemical.

Blueberries are often called huckleberries, but huckleberries are smaller and have larger seeds (and more taste). They are not cultivated.

Blueberries are best eaten with cream or in a dessert.

Cherries

There are innumerable varieties of cherry, and they are said to originate from two primitive species: the sweet cherry from Persia and Armenia, and the sour cherry, its origins unknown. Some cherries ripen in May, others not until late August or early September. Early settlers brought the cherry to the United States, and they were cultivated in New England and California. They may be golden-colored, blood red, deep red, sweet, or sour. The sweet cherries are used for eating, while the sour ones are cooked.

When you buy cherries, choose fresh-looking ripe ones and discard any that are bruised or wrinkled. Wash under running water and drain well.

Cherries can be cooked with veal, fish, chicken, and game and can be used in the preparation of jams, jellies, and desserts.

Cranberries

Cranberries are the fruit of a low, creeping evergreen plant that is native to North America. They were used by the Indians both for eating and for medicinal purposes. They are also related to the lingonberry of Sweden and can be successfully used in recipes calling for that particular berry. Cranberries were not cultivated until the nineteenth century, and now much the same methods are used for picking and sorting as were used at that time.

To test if a cranberry is a good one, see if it will bounce. If it does, it is good. If not, it will be overripe and mushy, or not ripe at all.

Cranberries can be used in many dishes in which their taste will change completely, such as cooked in stews or soups. They are also served with the perennial turkey, used as sauces and preserves.

Currants

Currants are native to Europe, Asia, and America, growing in the colder regions. There are various types, the best known being red, black, and white. Currants were brought to the United States by English settlers. Black currants are not common in the United States, although in Europe they are popular in Scandinavia, France, and England; in France they are used to make the blackberry liqueur, cassis. Red and white currants are used in jellies, jams, and desserts.

They should be washed thoroughly while they are still on the stalks. Do not remove them from the stalks until you are ready to use them. Pull the berries off the stalks with a fork.

Dates

Dates are the fruit of the date palm, one of the world's oldest plants, the origin of which is unknown. They are cultivated in Arab countries and in the United States. In the 1890s they were first brought to the United States for commercial production. Artificial pollination is necessary since the male and female principles grow on different trees.

The dates contain half their weight in sugar, and they are extremely nourishing. They provide food for the wandering tribes of the desert, and wines and spirits are made from them.

The fruit is about the size of the thumb and has a yellow-brown skin. To prepare them for cooking, remove the stones. They can be frozen. Do not buy dates that look old and dry.

Figs

Figs are the fruit of the fig tree and almost certainly came from the East. They were mentioned in the Bible and were not brought to the New World until the Spaniards arrived in South America. They are available from May to September but are very perishable and hard to transport. There are four kinds of figs on the market in the United States: the Calimyrna, which has a greenish-yellow skin and a sweet nutlike taste; the Black Mission, which is almost black when ripe; the Kadota fig, a light yellow fig; and the Brown Turkey, which is at its best when the fig is reddish brown.

Fresh figs are generally eaten raw. In *French Provincial Cooking* Elizabeth David says, "To the fortunate it occurs every now and then to bite into the sweet purple flesh of the fig as it is ready to crack through the bright green skin. . . ." I can almost taste it.

Recipes using apricots are also suitable for figs. When you choose them, they should be firm but with "give."

Gooseberries

Native to colder parts of Europe, Asia, and the Americas, the gooseberry is a large green berry streaked with red or white. In France it is called *groseille à maquereau* because it was traditionally served with mackerel. It has been cultivated in England since the early sixteenth century. Unfortunately, it is not widely cultivated in the United States. In 1898 it was said to have brought in a fungus that killed white pine trees and was outlawed in many states.

Choose fresh, firm-looking gooseberries. To prepare them, top and tail them with a pair of kitchen scissors or a small knife. They can be cooked with fish or goose, or as sauces or desserts. If fresh gooseberries are out of the question, canned ones can be substituted.

Grapes

Grapes are among the oldest known fruits. Noah is said to have first cultivated the vine, and vineyards were certainly grown long before the Bible was written. Grape vines grew wild in Europe and Asia Minor and were found wild in America. There are many different kinds of grapes, far too many to list, but the ones most common are the black and the green seedless grape. Green ones are used in classic French dishes bearing the name Veronique. (See page 79 for Sole Veronique, page 82 for Chicken Veronique, and page 118 for Tongue Veronique.)

Grapes are pressed to make wine and grape juice. During prohibition days some American wineries, confined to the manufacture of grape juice, were known to have stuck a label on the bottles that read: "Caution. This grape juice may ferment and become alcoholic."

The fresh juice from sour grapes, known as verjuice, can be used instead of vinegar. Dried grapes make raisins, currants, and sultanas.

To buy grapes choose ones that are heavy for their size and unwrinkled. Wash very thoroughly in running water and keep refrigerated.

Grapefruit

An ancestor of the grapefruit is believed to have been cultivated in the Malay archipelago for 2,000 years. Grapefruit came to the United States in the seventeenth century. It comes with both a pink and a yellow flesh inside. The habit of eating grapefruit before a meal was started by the Chinese and copied by the Americans. Eaten in conjunction with certain other foods on a high protein diet, it will accelerate weight loss. It is also high in vitamin C.

Buy grapefruit that is heavy for its size and thin-skinned. Chill before serving. To serve, cut it in half and with a curved serrated grapefruit knife cut around the rim and between the sections. It is also good in salads and desserts.

Guavas

The guava is the fruit of the guava tree, which grows mainly in tropical regions of Latin America and Asia. It is also cultivated in Hawaii, Florida, and Southern California. There are several species, which range from green to yellow-red in color and can be pear-, orange-, or fig-shaped.

Guavas can be stewed and made into jam, jelly, or pastes. Fresh guavas can be stewed and the purée sieved and made into fruit drinks or put into sauces. Canned guavas are more common than fresh ones. If fresh ones are available, choose firmer ones for cooking and ones that "give" slightly when pressed for eating.

Kiwi Fruit

Kiwi fruit comes from New Zealand and is occasionally available in Amercan markets. It is sometimes known as Chinese gooseberry, although its only resemblance would be in the color of its inside flesh. The fruit is about the size of a small lime. It has a thin furry brown skin outside, and when you slice it in half, you find a shiny emerald-green flesh inside with tiny black seeds and veins running around the center. The taste is something between a watermelon and a strawberry.

The fruit is high in vitamin C. Like papaya, it acts as a natural tenderizer when rubbed on meat. It is good in fresh fruit salads.

Kumquats

The kumquat has been grown for centuries in China. It is a citrus fruit, orange-yellow in color, small and oval-shaped, with a strong orange taste. The skin is sweet, and the meat is tart, quite the opposite of the orange.

Although you can sometimes get it fresh, you are more likely to come across it preserved in syrup. It is available this way in Chinese shops. It is delicious by itself or cooked with lamb and chicken.

Lemons

Lemons are the fruit of the lemon tree and are believed to have come originally from India. They have been cultivated for thousands of years. Commercial production is big in the Mediterranean and California. The fruit is highly scented and very acid. It contains plenty of vitamin C.

A sweet variety of lemon is grown in Latin America and the Orient, but the acid kind, brought to America by Columbus, is the kind mainly sold in the United States.

The juice and the peel of the lemon are used in all kinds of cooking, sweet and savory. Lemons have a special affinity for fish, enhance the flavor of sauces and salad dressings, and make excellent drinks and delicious desserts. Lemon juice will also prevent fruit or vegetables such as bananas, apples, or artichokes from going brown when they are exposed to the air.

When buying lemons, choose ones that are thin-skinned and heavy for their size. Keep refrigerated.

Lichee Fruit

A small, delicate oval-shaped Chinese fruit, lichee nuts have a reddish-brown rough-textured skin. They look a bit like giant strawberries, but the outer skin is hard. When they are peeled, the inside looks somewhat like a large peeled white grape. The pulp is translucent and juicy, and inside it you find a smooth brown seed. Fresh ones are available from May to August and can be kept 2 to 3 weeks. To buy them, choose firm fruits that are free of decay at the stem end.

They are most frequently sold canned and can be used with Chinese savory chicken, duck and pork dishes, or in sweet dishes.

Limes

Limes are a close cousin of the lemon and are also native to India and Southeast Asia. They came to the New World with Columbus, but since they require a hot tropical climate, they are not cultivated as widely as the lemon. Limes are often imported from Mexico and the West Indies.

Limes can be used in place of lemons.

Mangoes

Mangoes originated in India and have been cultivated in Southeast Asia for over 4,000 years. They grow on large trees as high as 40 to 50 feet. The fruit hangs from long stems; when it ripens, there is usually food for everyone, and mangoes are picked off the roadsides by anyone who feels like it.

Since mangoes only grow in hot climates, they are not grown in the United States except in Florida and Hawaii. They vary greatly in size and shape. Some are oval, some flat, some round. The smaller types tend to be stringy, while the larger ones are smooth and more delicate. When they are ripe, they have an apricot-colored flesh and are very juicy.

Buy unripe mangoes (since that is how they are usually sold) and let them ripen at room temperature. Do not be put off by speckles on the outer skin; they do not affect the fruit inside. To prepare them, peel from the small end of the fruit and slice the flesh away from the seed. Unripe green mangoes can be sliced and eaten with a little salt and chili. Ripe mangoes are delicious in curries and spicy dishes, with shrimp, and in sweet dishes.

Melons

Melons are a member of the cucumber family. They originated in Asia and were transplanted to Italy, then to France before the sixteenth century. Among the many varieties available in the United States, the best known are the honeydew and the cantaloupe. The honeydew has a pale greenish-yellow flesh and the cantaloupe a pale orange flesh. They are high in vitamins A and C.

To buy melon, choose one heavy for its size. The melon should smell good, and the end opposite the stem end should be slightly soft. Chill melon before serving. It is excellent by itself with sugar or salt and pepper. Lemon juice and ginger are also good seasonings. It takes its place as both an appetizer and a dessert.

Nectarines

Nectarines are a variety of peach, smooth-skinned and with a firmer flesh. Use them as peaches.

Oranges

Oranges are native to China and were introduced to Europe at the time of the Crusades. They were not developed commercially in the United States until the seventeenth century. There are many varieties of orange, including the bitter orange, mandarin orange with its thin, loose peel, and the tangerine. Most oranges in the United States come from California and Florida.

When you buy oranges, choose those that are heavy for their size, with a thin rather than a thick peel. The color of the skin has nothing to do with the quality of the orange. Oranges in their natural form often have green patches that appear if there is a spell of very hot weather. In the United States orange skins are treated with a chemical substance to make them look a brighter orange than they actually are. In fact, Americans are so used to this unlikely hue that in certain plush hotels in Mexico oranges are served already peeled so that tourists will not see the greenness of the outer skin and think that the orange is of poor quality. If you are using orange peel, then, try to get organically grown oranges because the chemicals are impossible to wash out.

Papayas

Grown for centuries by the Indians of Mexico and South America, the papaya is a large oblong-shaped fruit with a thick green or yellow skin and orange flesh. It is a common breakfast fruit in Latin America and is eaten with lemon or lime juice squeezed on the flesh. It is high in vitamins A and C, low in calories. Papayas are grown in Florida and Hawaii, but only the small, tough ones ship well. To taste a perfect papaya, you have to go to the region in which they are grown.

To buy papayas, if you want a ripe one, choose one that is soft to the touch and seems almost rotten. Unripe ones will mature if left on a windowsill.

Papaya contains papain, an enzyme that aids in the digestion of foods. It is also used as a meat tenderizer. Meat wrapped in papaya leaves and rubbed with the seeds or flesh will become tender.

Peaches

Peaches are said to have originated in China and came to Europe via Persia over 2,000 years ago. They were brought to the United States by the early settlers. Two types of peaches are available, one with a juicy flesh and freestone and the other with a firm flesh and clingstone. French peaches are among the best in the world.

Peaches should be eaten only in season. Off-season, they have been refrigerated and shipped so much that they are virtually tasteless. In season, peaches are often sold unripe because of shipping. Unfortunately, this robs the peach of much of its flavor; moreover, buying an unripe peach in the hope that it will ripen on the windowsill can be a chancy business. Slightly unripe peaches should be cooked. They are delicious with poultry and game or as a dessert.

To peel peaches, drop them for a few minutes in boiling water and slip the skins off.

Pears

Pears have been cultivated since Greek and Roman times and first came to the United States with the early settlers. There are endless varieties, and they include cooking and eating pears. In France and America pears can be bought for almost the entire year, from July to May. They vary greatly in variety, texture, color, and flavor. To test pears for ripeness, press very gently at the stalk end of the fruit. If you press in the middle, you will bruise the pear. It is hard to judge when a pear is at its perfect moment. The fruit often goes from ripeness to overripeness in a few hours. Although nutritionists will scream that the vitamins and minerals are mainly in its skin, a peeled pear does taste better than an un-peeled one.

Cooking pears have a firm flesh and are sometimes a little granular. They are more tart than eating pears. Dessert pears are good eaten raw and in sweets or preserves. Cooking pears are delicious in savory dishes and if overripe are excellent in sauces.

Persimmons

Persimmons were cultivated for centuries in Japan and China. They were brought to the United States in the early nineteenth century. The small fruit looks a bit like a tomato, with a bright orange-red skin. Two varieties are available: the Hachiya, with a slightly pointed shape and bright orange color, which is soft when ripe; and the Fuyu, which is flatter in shape and ready to eat while still firm.

If persimmons are eaten when they are green, they taste tart and puckery. They can be bought unripe and left to ripen on a windowsill. They can be eaten raw or stewed.

Pineapples

Pineapples are native to the Americas and originated in Brazil and Paraguay. They are now cultivated all over Asia and Africa and are provided for the United States market by Hawaii, Mexico, and the Caribbean.

To test if a pineapple is ripe, thump it; if it has a heavy, dull sound, it is probably ripe. It should have a sweet smell and should be heavy for its size. The top leaves should not be dried, and the pineapple should be yellow with a greenish top color. Pineapples that are picked green never taste as good as those allowed to ripen on the stem.

The juice of fresh pineapples is very good for digestion, especially so after a meal containing a lot of meat. Pineapples can be cooked with duck, shrimp, and chicken, or eaten cooked or raw as a dessert.

Plums

Plums originated in Southwest Asia and came to the United States through Europe. There are several varieties, the best of which is the Greengage, or Reine Claude, named after Queen Claude, daughter of Louis XII and wife of Frances I. Damson plums are particularly good for jams and preserves and are best eaten cooked.

Plums must be ripe when they are bought, otherwise they taste bitter and unpleasant; even when cooked they will taste mediocre. Cooked plums are good in sweet or savory sauces, in soups, and cooked with game. They are also good as a dessert, stewed with sugar and served with cream. Dried plums are sold as prunes.

Pomegranates

The pomegranate is one of the most ancient of fruits. It is mentioned in the Bible, in Sanskrit writings, and in Homer's *Odyssey*. It originates in North Africa. The fruit is about the size of an orange, and it has a tough skin which ranges in color from light yellow to purplish red. Inside, the pulp is red and contains numerous seeds. Grenadine, the flavoring for drinks, is made from pomegranate juice. You can make your own by straining the juice through a cheesecloth.

Pomegranates are usually picked before they are ripe because they are inclined to split if allowed to ripen on the tree. They should have a thin, tough rind and a dark red color. The large sizes have juicier kernels. You can keep the fruit for several weeks at room temperature. The seeds can be used in stuffings and garnishes.

Quinces

The quince is a relative of the pear and grows on a small shrublike tree that belongs to the rose family. It originated in Persia and Greece and came to the United States with the early settlers. It is a round or pear-shaped fruit that resembles an apple. It is excellent cooked with other foods, stewed as a dessert, or made into jellies or preserves, but it is not good eaten raw.

To buy quinces, which are in season from October to December, choose those that are smooth and unblemished, without spots and bruises. Keep them in a cold, dry place.

Raspberries

Raspberries are the fruit of the bramble bush, which grows wild in temperate climates of Europe, Asia, and North America. Many varieties are cultivated, and they vary in color from black, red, and purple to pink and yellow.

Raspberries are extremely delicate and travel badly. Unfortunately, they are extremely expensive as a result. Although they are available everywhere in Europe during the summer, they are sold at outrageous prices in tiny little half-pints in many parts of the United States. The only way to enjoy this fruit, I suppose, is to grow it yourself.

Apart from eating raspberries raw with a little sugar and cream, they can also be made into sauces, desserts, jams, and jellies. A superb brandy and liqueur is distilled from them.

Rhubarb

Rhubarb is not a fruit, but the stalk of a wide-leafed plant. There are many species, and it is believed to have originated in northern Asia and brought to Europe in the fourteenth century. The roots have been used for medicine in China since the third century and were originally used as medicine by European monks. Rhubarb was then an ornamental plant; it was not until the seventeenth century that the stalks were eaten.

The leaves of the rhubarb plant are poisonous. To prepare it, discard the leaves and wash the rhubarb stalks thoroughly. Cut them into 2-inch pieces. The rhubarb can then be stewed, baked, or made into preserves.

Strawberries

The strawberry plant is a member of the rose family and is common throughout Europe and America. Indians were cultivating strawberries in South America long before the Spaniards arrived. They are easy to grow and have been cultivated in the United States since the early nineteenth century. There are many varieties.

When you buy strawberries, avoid those glossy fat strawberries the size of golf balls. They are woolly and tasteless inside. Avoid strawberries that are moldy or blemished. Wash them very thoroughly, for they are sprayed not only when they grow but several times after they are picked to stop them from going moldy. The best strawberries of all, in my opinion, are wild *fraises des bois*.

Strawberries can be made into soups, sauces, jams, and jellies and eaten as dessert.

Tangerines

The tangerine is the fruit of a species of orange tree and originates in China. It is cultivated in the southern United States and is usually eaten raw. Sections of peeled tangerine are good for garnishing food, particularly desserts or sweet-sour dishes. Dried tangerine peel is frequently used as a flavoring in Chinese dishes. It must be soaked first.

15

Watermelon

Like other melons, watermelon is a member of the cucumber family. It is believed to have originated in Africa and is mentioned in ancient Sanskrit and Arabic writings. It has been grown for hundreds of years in Russia and in the Middle East. There are many varieties of watermelon, and it comes with white, yellow, or red flesh. Sometimes it has a pleasant musky flavor; at other times it is rather tasteless.

Eaten raw, watermelon is an excellent thirst quencher during the summer. It makes a good light dessert, but it is usually better mixed with other fruits. Pickled watermelon rind is a great delicacy. The dried roasted seeds can be eaten like nuts or used in sweet dishes.

About Nuts

Millions of people in the tropics depend on nuts to keep them alive. They are the richest source of fat and protein, containing more protein than meat or fish. They are especially good eaten at the end of a meal, for they clean the teeth.

Many of the nuts sold in the United States are grown in the United States. Almonds come from California; walnuts and hazelnuts from California, Oregon, and Washington; macadamia nuts from Hawaii; pine nuts from the Southwest. Pistachios come from the Middle East; Brazil nuts from South America; cashews from India and Africa; coconuts from the West Indies, Central America, and the Philippines; and chestnuts from Europe. Peanuts are grown in the United States.

When you buy nuts, avoid any that are split, cracked, or stained. Ask the vendor how long he has held them. If they have been sitting around at room temperature for a long time, they may be stale and rancid.

Most nuts sold in their shells are not roasted. Shelled nuts are sold roasted, raw, or blanched, and if roasted are often salted and spiced. They are also sold ground, in broken pieces, in slivers, or whole.

Avoid salted, roasted nuts. They have usually been roasted in hydrogenated fats and are oversalted. Not only are home-roasted nuts better for you, they also taste better. (See page 39.) Avoid ready-ground nuts; they have about as much food value as sawdust. You can pulverize nuts in a mortar, a coffee grinder, or a food mill; in a special nut mill; or in a blender. Ground nuts are excellent for flavoring sauces, soups, and stews.

Nuts in their shell have far more texture and flavor than shelled nuts, but for cooking purposes, unless you have someone to do it for you, the time and labor involved shelling them is not worth it. And when you are trying to keep them whole, they often break.

Nut butters are extremely good in sauces and stews. They can be served in rice or over vegetables. Avoid those made with hydrogenated fats.

Nuts should be stored in a cool, dry place, preferably the refrigerator. High temperatures make the fat in the nuts go rancid. To keep them fresh, store them in closed containers. Nuts in their shells last longer than shelled ones; unroasted ones last longer than roasted ones. Nuts can be successfully frozen. Chestnuts can be blanched, shelled, and frozen.

Chop blanched nuts while they are still hot. It is much easier.

Almonds

The almond is the fruit of the almond tree, a member of the peach family. There are two varieties, sweet and bitter, the sweet almond being the one most commonly found in the shops today. They are one of the earliest-known nuts, mentioned in the Bible and in early histories. Romans called the almonds "Greek nuts," which suggests that they may have originally come from Greece, although they have been cultivated along the Mediterranean coast for centuries. Today, they are grown in Italy, in the Provence and Languedoc regions of France, in North Africa, and in California.

Almonds are one of the richest sources of protein. They are high in vitamins A and B, phosphorus, magnesium, and potassium. They contain 21 per cent protein, and more than half their weight is oil, which is a source of essential fatty acid. The oil can be used in cooking and on salads. Ground almonds are extremely good for thickening sauces. They also make wonderful soup (page 31). Slivered almonds are used in classic French cuisine with trout and string beans. Chopped or ground, their subtle sweet flavor will enhance almost any dish.

Almonds are sold in their shells, whole and shelled, slivered, chopped, or ground. They are, of course, freshest when in their shells. However, whole almonds with their skins on are quite satisfactory for cooking. Blanched almonds do not have so much flavor. If they must be blanched, it is better to do it yourself by dropping them into boiling water and slipping off their skins. Of course you will be losing many minerals and vitamins, but for some dishes skinned almonds are definitely preferable. Avoid preground or chopped almonds; they have very little taste. If you have a blender or a food mill, it does not take long to grind them or chop them yourself.

Brazil Nuts

Brazil nuts are grown in Paraguay and Brazil. They were not discovered by the United States until after the Second World War, although they were first exported to Europe in 1633. Now the United States buys half the quantity exported.

Contrary to common belief, the Brazil nut is not a nut at all but a seed. The actual nut, which comes from trees as high as 150 feet, with trunks as wide as 6 feet around, is the size of a coconut. Inside are packed the seeds, little triangular-shaped shells, brown and white in color. These are what we know as Brazil nuts. The forests of Brazil contain millions of these trees, and to see them one must feel like a dwarf in a land of giants. They are not cultivated, but their propagation is carried out by the Amazonian hare, which, like our native squirrel, collects and stores his nuts for future use. Those he forgets lie buried in the ground and eventually grow into trees, which become fully grown in about 9 years. When the nuts are ripe, tropical storms gather and rip through the jungle, hurling the nuts to the ground. Each tree yields about 600 to 1,000 pounds of Brazil nuts.

Brazil nuts contain 17 per cent protein. They are sometimes crushed and turned into oil. They are used for confectionery, and of course they turn up every year on the Christmas table. They always seem to be the last nuts to leave the bowl because they are extremely hard to crack. When you do crack them, there is always a stubborn little piece that refuses to come out. If you bake them in the oven first, the shells will split more easily. You can buy the nuts already shelled, but of course the flavor will be less pronounced, and they will be more expensive. They are good ground as flavorings, chopped for stuffings, and sprinkled on meat or vegetable dishes. If they are not available, hazelnuts can be used instead.

Cashew Nuts

The cashew nut originated in Brazil. It was exported by the Portuguese in the sixteenth century, and it is now grown all over the tropics. It is grown on the pear-cashew tree, which bears a juicy red or yellow fruit. The nut is attached to the end, like a large olive-colored kidney bean, and inside is the kernel, a sweet white nut.

In Brazil the juice of the cashew pear is fermented for wine and vinegar.

In the West Indies the juice is used for jelly or soft drinks. The nuts are cooked in curries, stews, fried dishes, and sauces. They can also be chopped and sprinkled on a dish after it has been cooked.

Cashew nuts are sold shelled and, more often than not, salted and washed. Avoid the salted ones if possible. Unroasted nuts are available in health food stores. They taste much better if you roast them yourself.

Chestnuts

Chestnuts grow inside prickly shells on large trees, some as high as 100 feet with trunks 6 to 12 feet in diameter. Until 1900 they grew all over the eastern United States, but they were attacked by a virulent fungus and by the 1930s were almost nonexistent. In Europe, however, the chestnut tree still survives, and the nuts are available throughout the fall and winter months. Do not buy them at other times of the year because they do not keep.

Italians and Chinese dry the chestnuts to preserve them. To use them, soak them for a few hours in water and simmer for 2 hours in 5 cups of water per pound. Remove the dark outer skin. Dried chestnuts give a delicious rich smoky taste to meat and chicken dishes. A flour is also made from chestnuts.

Fresh chestnuts can be eaten as a vegetable, boiled, steamed, glazed, puréed, or as a sauce or a dessert. They make an excellent stuffing for goose or turkey.

Coconut

Coconut is the fruit of the tall, graceful tropical palm tree, and it is grown all over the tropics. If coconuts are gathered before they are ripe, they are green and contain jelly and water. Ripe ones are brown and have a hollow center, less milk, and a thick white flesh that adheres to the shell.

In the Caribbean green coconuts are sold as a refreshing drink. Coconut venders tap the shells and can tell by the sound how much milk they contain, and they charge accordingly.

The white meat of the ripe coconut is known as copra, and it is used for a vast variety of products, including fat, soap, candles, and margarine. It can be grated, toasted, or flaked and the milk made into cream. Fresh grated coconut can be frozen indefinitely in a tightly sealed container. Grated coconut or coconut milk can be added to stews and curries and gives them a distinctive and attractive flavor. It is also used in sweet dishes, candies, puddings, and cakes.

When you buy coconuts, choose those that are heavy for their size. To open them, see page 131.

Hazelnuts

Hazelnuts grow surrounded by a tight little cluster of leaves on small bushes or trees of the birch family. These brown nuts are also known as filberts because they ripen around St. Philbert's Day, August 22. They are rich in oil and protein.

Lightly roasted, the nuts make a delicious butter (page 128), which is used in French cooking for hors d'oeuvres and for soups and white sauces. They can be ground in a blender or food mill and stored in a tightly sealed container in the refrigerator. They are excellent in sauces, with meat, or chopped and sprinkled over vegetables.

They are sold both shelled and unshelled. Either will do, although the shelled ones will taste fresher.

Macadamia Nuts

Named after John Macadam, a seventeenth-century Scottish scientist, these are the fruit of a small tree or shrub that was discovered in Australia. They grow in southern Asia and Hawaii as well.

They are usually sold in small jars or cans, and they are very expensive in most parts of the United States. They are not cheap even in Hawaii. They are generally sold as cocktail nuts, already salted. They are delicious in Southeast Asian saté dishes and with meat, fish, or chicken.

Peanuts

Peanuts are a legume, a member of the pea and bean family, not a nut, as is commonly believed. The pods grow below the surface of the earth to mature the seeds, which are then eaten either raw or toasted. The nut is also known as the monkey nut or ground nut.

Peanuts came originally from Brazil. The Portuguese took the nuts to West Africa, and from there they spread all over the tropics and grow in all hot countries today. Three common varieties are grown in the United States: the Virginia, which is long and slender; the runner, which is small and stubby; and the Spanish peanut, which is small and round. Peanuts have considerable nutritional value, containing 30 per cent protein.

Most peanuts in the United States are sold already roasted, even when in their shells. To make them taste even better, roast them again (in their shells). They will taste even fresher and make a delicious peanut butter. Combine the shelled roasted nuts in a blender with a little peanut oil and blend until you have a paste. It is a vast improvement over store-bought peanut butter, and it does not contain harmful hydrogenated fat. Homemade peanut butter is delicious on toast with lettuce, tarragon, or parsley, or with ham. It also makes a very good sauce (page 124) for tongue and other cold meats. Peanuts are also good cooked with chicken, fish, and meat.

Pecans

The pecan, with its graceful, long smooth brown shell, is the most popular nut in the United States. It is a species of American hickory, discovered wild by the Indians. It was mentioned in 1519 by explorers who found the Indians using it as a seasoning, cooking it in corncakes and hominy, extracting oil from it, and using it as a drink. It grows in the South and Midwest, Georgia being its prime producer. The early French settlers in Louisiana made the famous praline from it, and pecan pie has become a famous American classic. It is often brought out with its sister, pumpkin pie, at Thanksgiving dinners.

Pecans are sold both shelled and in their shells, which are very easy to crack. Its rich, sweet, delicate flavor goes with fish, chicken, and veal and in sauces as well as in the better-known desserts.

Pine Nuts

Also known as pignolia and piñon nut, the pine nut is the kernel of the cone of the stone pine and is grown in Italy and in the Southwest of the United States. It is about ¼ inch long, a cream-colored oily nut with a delicate flavor. In the Southwest the wonderful scent of piñon pervades the air. The Indians use the nut for soups, as a paste for cakes, in sauces, and in salads. In Italy it is used primarily in meat and game dishes and as the basis for the superb pesto (page 67) for spaghetti. It can also be fried and salted (page 39) and served with drinks. It often finds its way into the confectionery and cakes of the Italians.

In the Middle East and Latin America pine nuts are used frequently as stuffings for meat or fish.

Both imported and domestic pine nuts are available in the United States. I really see no reason to spend a lot of money on a tiny bottle of imported pine nuts when one can get the same thing loose at a quarter the price—and just as good. Store them in tightly sealed jars.

Pistachios

The little green-flecked nut grows on pistachio trees in the Mediterranean coast, Asia Minor, and Persia. When it is in bloom, a strong sweet smell pervades the whole region. Iran produces the biggest and sweetest nuts and is the main exporter.

In India and the Middle East they are used with rice, in soups and stews, and in chicken, fish, and meat dishes. They also form the basis of those superb syrup-soaked cakes and candies that are just as popular in the West now as they are in the East. In the United States pistachios are mixed into ice cream, sherbet, and nougat.

Pistachios are usually sold roasted and salted. If it is possible, buy them at a Middle Eastern, Greek, or Indian shop. You may find them in large 2-pound bags, which are not expensive compared with the price you pay for those little plastic bags in a supermarket. The nuts should be stored in the refrigerator.

Walnuts

The walnut, which is as versatile a nut for cooking as the almond, is found in Europe and America, the fruit of the walnut tree. It was known by the Greeks four centuries before Christ, and its cultivation was extended all over Europe by the Romans.

ABOUT NUTS

The French and Italian walnuts are the best. In Mexico I had tiny walnuts no bigger than hazelnuts, and they were among the best I have ever tasted. They were sweet and fresh and had none of the bitterness of the large overgrown walnuts that are sometimes on the market. Buy walnuts early in the season while the flavor is still strong and fresh. If they are left exposed to the air for too long, the kernels shrink, and taste is lost.

Walnut oil, which comes primarily from France, has a haunting smoky flavor that is especially delicious in salads. It was once used mainly for painting, but few painters thought to taste it.

Walnuts can be ground and used in sauces, chopped over fish and eggs, in salads, or in stuffings.

Soup

Soups made with fruits or nuts are light and delicate and are becoming increasingly popular in the United States. Served cold, they are particularly refreshing as a noontime drink during a hot summer day, as a cool beginning to a curry or spicy meal, or as a summer supper when it's too hot for anything else. Hot fruit soups are a good light beginning to a winter meal.

In Germany and Russia fruit soups are often served hot with semolina dumplings, sour cream, or rusks as a lunch or supper dish. Mediterranean, Latin American, and Middle Eastern cooking contains much in the way of nut soups, many of which are served with cream and lemon as the beginning of a meal.

Fruit soups can be served cold as dessert, and they are also delicious as a hot bedtime drink during the winter.

Cold Berry Soup

On a hot summer day this soup is an excellent noontime dish. It is even better made a day ahead of time so that the flavors have time to develop.

1½   pounds fresh strawberries or raspberries
½   cup sugar
2   cups water
1   cup red wine
    Juice of half a lemon
    Rind of half a lemon, grated
½   cup sour cream

Wash the berries and rub them through a sieve. Bring the sugar and water to boil in a saucepan and make a syrup. Cool. Combine the berries, syrup, red wine, lemon juice, and rind and mix together in a large bowl.

Correct sweetening. Chill. Before serving, put about a tablespoon of sour cream in each dish.

Serves about 4.

Basic Fruit Soup or Stock

Very ripe and overripe fruits can be used for this soup. You can make it with almost any combination of fruit, whatever happens to be in season. In Israel this soup is eaten with boiled potatoes.

It is also an excellent base for sauces, meat, and poultry dishes that call for stock (particularly curry and highly spiced dishes) and as a light summer meal.

Vary the quantities as you please.

2   oranges, peeled and sliced
2   apples, peeled, cored, and sliced
2   apricots, pitted
2   peaches, pitted
4   plums, pitted
    Some grapes or cherries, pitted
    About 3 pints water
    Cinnamon
    Lemon or orange peel
    Cloves
    Sugar to taste

Bring the fruit to a boil in the water with spices and sugar and simmer for about 15 minutes or until the fruit is soft.

Makes about 8 cups.

Cranberry Apple Soup

Serve with sour cream and rusks (hard, crisp bread).

1   pound cranberries
1   cup sugar
1   pound cooking apples, peeled, cored, and sliced
5   cups water
1   tablespoon cornstarch mixed with 1 tablespoon water

Simmer cranberries in the water for 10 minutes. Strain through a sieve, pressing down on the berries to extract all the juice.

Return the juice to the pan with the sugar and apples. Bring to boil, thicken with cornstarch, and chill.

Serves 4 to 6.

Cherry Soup

This soup is popular in Russia and Germany as well as in France, and it is good either as a beginning or as an end to a meal. Serve it with sour cream and rusks.

1 pound cherries
3 cups water
   Cinnamon stick
1 tablespoon lemon peel
4 cloves
1 cup red wine (preferably Bordeaux)
1 tablespoon cornstarch mixed with 1 tablespoon water
2–3 tablespoons sugar
   Lemon juice to taste

Simmer the cherries in 1 cup water with the cinnamon, lemon peel, and cloves for 10 minutes. Remove the stones and sieve half the cherries. Add the remaining water and bring to boil.

Meanwhile, crush the cherry stones in a mortar and bring to boil with the wine. Strain through a cheesecloth and add. (You can omit this step and just add the wine.) Add the cornstarch and sugar and simmer until thick. Add lemon juice and extra sugar if necessary.

Serves 4.

Note: A blueberry soup can be successfully made the same way.

Soupa Avgolémono

This is a famous Greek lemon soup. Once you have added the eggs to it, you must be ready to serve it right away. If it is overcooked, it will be ruined.

6 cups chicken broth
⅓ cup rice
2 egg yolks
1 large lemon
   Coarse salt and freshly ground white pepper

Bring the broth to the boil and add the rice. Turn heat down and simmer gently until the rice is cooked. Whisk the egg yolks with the lemon juice and add about a cup of the boiling broth gradually, bit by bit, to the egg mixture, stirring all the time. Add this to the rest of the broth, stirring continuously, and cook over very low heat for a few minutes. Season with salt and pepper, turn into heated soup plates, and serve immediately.

Enough for 4.

Cranberry Borscht

1	onion, chopped
1	ounce butter
1	1-pound can beets
1½	pints chicken or veal stock
1	pound cranberries
¼	cup Madeira or dry sherry
	Lemon juice to taste
	Coarse salt and freshly ground pepper
	Sour cream
	Chopped fresh chives

Soften the onion in the butter. Drain and chop the beets, reserving the juice. Purée in blender with the onions and the beet juice.

Combine stock and cranberries in another pan and simmer for 10 minutes. Purée in blender and sieve.

Add to the beet purée and mix well. Add Madeira, lemon juice, and correct seasoning. Serve hot or cold with sour cream and chives to garnish.

Serves 4.

Cold Plum Soup

This is an excellent hot-weather soup, good for lunch or as a dessert.

2	pounds tart red plums
4	cups water
	Sugar to taste
	Lemon juice to taste
1–2	teaspoons arrowroot
	Sour cream to garnish

Simmer the plums in the water until they are soft. Sieve them and return the purée to the saucepan. Add sugar and lemon juice. Mix the arrowroot with a little of the liquid to make a smooth paste and add. Stir well and bring to boil. Simmer until thickened to the consistency of light cream. Cool and refrigerate (preferably overnight). Serve garnished with sour cream.

Serves 4.

Orange-Tomato Soup

The first time I made this, I put in far too much orange juice. The oranges were rather sweet, and the result was very odd indeed. Unless you like to start a meal with a very sweet soup, I suggest you make sure that your oranges are fairly bitter and that you *taste as you cook*. Made correctly, this is delicious, especially during the summer when it is very good cold. It is good for lunch, followed by an omelette.

1½	pounds ripe tomatoes
½	cup orange juice (fresh, of course)
1½	cups meat or chicken stock
	Celery salt
	Celery leaves for flavoring (if available)
	Coarse salt and freshly ground black pepper
¼	cup dry sherry
4 to 6	tablespoons heavy cream

Peel the tomatoes and put them in a saucepan with the orange juice. Add the stock, celery salt, and leaves; season and simmer for about half an hour. Remove the leaves and purée the mixture in the blender. Correct seasoning. If you are serving the soup hot, return it to the stove and heat it through. When ready to serve, spoon a little sherry and heavy cream into each serving.

Enough for 4.

Asparagus and Almond Soup

2	pounds fresh asparagus
7	cups veal or chicken stock
¾	cup almonds, pulverized in a blender or food mill
	Coarse salt and freshly ground pepper
	Lemon juice to taste
2	tablespoons chopped fresh chives
6	tablespoons cream

Simmer the asparagus in the stock until tender. Remove and chop coarsely, reserving tips for garnish if you like. Put in blender with some of the stock and purée (or put through fine blade of a food mill).

Add the almonds and seasonings and bring to boil. Chill. Add lemon juice, chives, and cream.

Serves 6 to 8.

Raisin Vegetable Soup

This is a delicious light spring soup and should be made with new peas if you can get them. Frozen peas will do otherwise.

1	onion, finely chopped
3	tablespoons butter
1	cup shelled peas (or 1 package frozen)
½	cup young green beans, cut in small pieces
1½	pints chicken or veal stock
¼	cup raisins soaked for 1 hour in water
½	cup cooked rice
	Lemon juice to taste
	Coarse salt and freshly ground white pepper
4	tablespoons heavy cream
½	cup chopped nuts (almonds, hazelnuts, Brazil nuts, etc.)
2	tablespoons chopped fresh chives

Soften the onion in the butter and add the peas and beans. Cook for 2 minutes. Add the stock and simmer for 45 minutes.

Add the raisins, rice, and lemon juice to taste and simmer 10 minutes. Correct seasoning and add heavy cream. Garnish with nuts and chives and serve.

Serves 4.

Almond Soup

This is one of the most delicious soups I have tasted. It is light and delicate and not too filling before the main course.

1 ounce butter
1 medium onion, chopped
½ clove garlic, finely chopped
1 green pepper, chopped
1 cup ground almonds
4 cups chicken stock
  Freshly ground coriander seed
  Coarse salt and freshly ground pepper
2 egg yolks
1 teaspoon freshly grated lemon rind

Melt the butter in a saucepan. Soften the onion with the garlic, add the green pepper, and cook until soft. Add the remaining ingredients except the egg yolks and lemon rind and simmer for 20 minutes.

Remove from heat and add a small amount of the liquid to the egg yolks and mix. Then slowly add eggs to the warm soup and beat. Sprinkle with lemon rind and serve.

Serves 4 to 6.

Note: Almonds freshly pulverized in the blender will have much more taste than those ready ground.

Navy Bean and Almond Soup

This soup improves if it is made the day before. In this case you must start it two days early because the beans must be soaked overnight.

½ cup navy or white beans, soaked overnight in water
3 cups chicken stock
¾ cup skinned almonds
2 leeks, chopped
3 cloves garlic
½ cup white wine
  Coarse salt and freshly ground pepper
1 teaspoon sugar
  Lemon juice to taste
  Chopped fresh parsley to garnish

Simmer the beans in the chicken stock, covered, until they are cooked. Meanwhile, purée the almonds in a blender or with a mortar and pestle. When the beans are cooked, add them. Add the leeks. Mash the garlic to a paste in a mortar with a little salt. Add to the beans, together with the wine and seasonings.

Simmer until the leeks are cooked. Remove from stove and put through a sieve, food mill, or coarse blade of the blender. Add lemon juice. Chill and serve garnished with whole almonds and fresh parsley, finely chopped.

Serves 4.

Tomato Soup with Almonds

Tomatoes can be peeled easily if you roll them over a gas flame or drop them for one minute into boiling water.

    1   cup almonds
    5   cups veal or chicken stock
    1   onion
    1   ounce butter
    6   large tomatoes, peeled
        Bay leaf
        Coarse salt and freshly ground pepper
        Chopped fresh basil, tarragon, or parsley

Pulverize the almonds in a blender with a little stock or put them through a food mill. Soften the onion in the butter and add the tomatoes. Cook for 5 minutes. Add half the stock and put in blender or through food mill. Return to the saucepan with remaining stock and almonds. Add the bay leaf, salt, and pepper and simmer for 20 minutes. Remove bay leaf, sprinkle with fresh herbs, and serve.

Serves 4.

Chestnut Soup

To peel chestnuts, see page 57.

This soup can be served hot or cold, but it is better cold.

    1   pound chestnuts, peeled
    1   tablespoon butter
    1   onion, chopped
    1   pint chicken stock
        Bouquet garni (parsley, thyme, cloves, and bay leaf tied in cheesecloth)
        Coarse salt and freshly ground black pepper
    1   tablespoon dry sherry per serving (optional)
    ¼   pint cream

Chop the chestnuts coarsely and reserve about 2 tablespoons for garnishing the soup. In a saucepan heat the butter and cook the onion gently until it is clear. Add the chestnuts, cook for about 3 more minutes, and add the stock and *bouquet garni*. Simmer for about 20 minutes. Put in the blender (if you have one) until you have a thick soup with no lumps. Otherwise, put through a sieve (removing the *bouquet* in both cases, of course). Season and add the cream and sherry. Scatter the remaining chestnuts over and serve.

Serves 4.

Peanut Soup

½   pound shelled peanuts
1   onion, finely chopped
1½ ounces butter
4   cups chicken or beef stock
    Dash Tabasco sauce
    Coarse salt and freshly ground pepper
4   tablespoons thick cream
1   glass sherry or Madeira
2   tablespoons chopped fresh chives
    Hungarian paprika

Pulverize the nuts in a blender or food mill. Soften the onion in the butter and add the nuts. Cook for 2 minutes. Add the stock, Tabasco, and seasonings and simmer for 45 minutes. Remove from heat and stir in the cream and sherry. Sprinkle with chives and paprika and serve.

Serves 4.

Lentil and Pistachio Nut Soup

3   onions, chopped
2   tablespoons butter
2   carrots, chopped
2   stalks celery, plus leaves, chopped
2   cups lentils
3   pints chicken broth
    Coarse salt and freshly ground pepper
1   cup skinned pistachio nuts
    Paprika
    Chopped fresh coriander or parsley

Soften the onions in the butter. Add the carrots and celery and cook for 5 minutes without browning. Add the lentils and broth and simmer gently until the lentils are cooked. Purée either in a blender or food mill, or through a sieve. Season with salt and pepper.

Add the chopped pistachio nuts, heat through, and serve with paprika and coriander scattered over the top.

Serves 8.

Hors d'Oeuvres and Salads

There is no more delicious way to begin a meal than with a light and attractive dish that stimulates the appetite without being too filling before the main course arrives. Figs with Parma ham, melon with port, stuffed vine leaves, and chilled grapefruit cocktail are simple but excellent dishes. A meal can also be started with a small salad such as cold asparagus with walnut dressing or cucumbers stuffed with cashews.

Rich spicy food does not go well with drinks in the summer. With summer cocktails such as champagne, rum, and gin drinks, fruit is the most refreshing. It must be fresh and clean, not stale and woolly. Of course, fresh fruit—*really* fresh fruit—is extremely hard to come by these days unless you grow your own. Few things are more delicious with drinks outside on a summer evening than a large bowl of fresh strawberries accompanied by a bowl of sugar and thick cream. Fresh figs with Greek feta cheese, a bowl of cherries, pickled watermelon rind, and fresh green almonds all go beautifully with cold summer drinks, sangría, or chilled white wine.

Nuts are the established cocktail staple, and your own roasted salted nuts will be far superior to the store-bought ones. You can also keep a supply of chopped nuts in a sealed jar in the refrigerator to use on top of canapés or other cocktail tidbits.

As for salads, there are endless recipes that combine fruits and nuts with vegetables and cover the lot with a heavy mayonnaise. Ever since I was given canned peaches stuffed with frozen shrimp on iceberg lettuce doused with bottled mayonnaise as my first American lunch, I have had a strong aversion to this kind of salad. I do like light orange salads that go with duck or game or Middle Eastern food.

Sweet-Sour Cherries

Serve these like olives. They keep in a tightly sealed jar for about a year. Use the tart bright red morello cherries that are in season in August.

1 pound cherries
1 stick cinnamon
2 sprigs tarragon
2 cups wine vinegar
4 cloves
  Dash nutmeg
6 ounces white sugar

Shorten the stalks of the cherries and pierce each cherry with the point of a needle. Discard any rotten cherries. Put them in a jar with the cinnamon stick and tarragon.

Boil the vinegar with the cloves, nutmeg, and sugar, covered, for about 10 minutes. Let it get completely cold before you pour it on the cherries.

Use after a month.

Grilled Grapefruit

Choose a fruit that is heavy but with a thin skin. Cut the fruit in half and with a sharp knife (preferably a grapefruit knife or one with a serrated edge) cut between the sections and around the rim of the grapefruit so that the sections will come out easily with a spoon.

2 grapefruit
  Brown sugar
  About 2 tablespoons dry sherry
  Dash cinnamon
  Dash nutmeg, freshly grated

Prepare the grapefruit and scatter brown sugar over the top of each half. Add sherry and spices to each and put under a hot grill long enough for the top to brown and the sugar to melt into a syrup. Serve immediately.

Serves 4.

Grapefruit Cocktail

2 grapefruit
2 oranges
  Angostura bitters
  Brown sugar to taste
4 tablespoons rum

Halve the grapefruit and remove the segments, discarding the white pith and membrane. Peel the orange and divide into sections, removing the pith and membrane. Mix together and put back in the grapefruit shells. Sprinkle with bitters, brown sugar, and rum. Serve chilled.

Serves 4.

Grapefruit with Muscat Grapes

2	grapefruit
2	tablespoons chopped blanched almonds
¼	pound grapes, pipped
3	tablespoons olive oil
1	tablespoon lemon juice
1	tablespoon brown sugar
	Chopped fresh mint to garnish

Halve the grapefruit and remove the segments, discarding the white pith and membrane. Mix with the almonds and grapes and return to the grapefruit shells. Combine the remaining ingredients and pour on each serving. Sprinkle with chopped mint.

Serves 4.

Melon with Ginger

Cut a ripe melon in half if it is small or in large slices if it is large. Remove the seeds, cut between the flesh and the rind, and then cut down vertically, cutting the flesh into 1-inch pieces but keeping the shape of the slice intact. Serve with sugar and ginger on the table.

Melon with Port

Pour a little port on each slice and serve.

Melon with Prosciutto

Serve the melon with very thin slices of prosciutto on the side. A slice of lemon on the side is a nice addition.

Figs with Prosciutto

An Italian hors d'oeuvre. For each serving peel about 4 ripe figs, wrap a piece of thinly sliced prosciutto ham around each one, and sprinkle with freshly ground pepper. Serve with thin pieces of toast.

Dates with Prosciutto

Remove the pits from some soft dates and wrap each one in a thin slice of prosciutto, securing with a toothpick. Sprinkle with freshly ground pepper and hand round with drinks before the meal.

Stuffed Eggs with Chutney and Hazelnuts

Use any kind of fruit chutney for this recipe and scatter the nuts over the top. This dish also makes a good side dish to go with curries.

    6   eggs, hard-boiled
    4   tablespoons fruit chutney
    ½   cup shelled hazelnuts
         Coarse salt and freshly ground black pepper

Peel the eggs, cut them in half, and scoop out the yolks into a bowl. Mash them with the chutney. Roast the hazelnuts in the oven, chop, and add them to the mixture. Season and stuff into the egg whites.
    Makes 12 halves.

Walnut-Stuffed Eggs

Hard-boil half a dozen eggs. Cut them in half and remove the yolks. In a mixing bowl combine the yolks with half a cup of finely chopped walnuts, about 3 to 4 tablespoons Roquefort cheese (at room temperature), 12 black olives, pitted and chopped, and mix well. Stuff into the egg whites and garnish with slivers of pimiento, chopped parsley, and paprika.

Almond Cheese Balls

You can buy almonds already roasted and unsalted in a can. They are quite good and save time if you don't want to roast them yourself. Otherwise buy slivered almonds and roast them in the oven on a sheet of aluminum foil.

6   scallions
¼   pound cream cheese
½   pound blue cheese
2   tablespoons fresh, finely chopped parsley
½   cup roasted chopped almonds
    Paprika

Chop the scallions, including the green part, finely. Put in a mixing bowl with the cheeses, the parsley, and half the almonds. Mix well and form into tiny balls (about golf-ball size). Roll in the remaining almonds and scatter paprika over them.

Salted Nuts

Homemade salted nuts are infinitely superior to bought ones. They are also very simple to prepare. Almonds, hazelnuts, pistachios, walnuts, pecans, Brazil nuts, peanuts, and pine nuts can be used.

Almonds can be roasted with or without the skins. To peel them, blanch them by covering with boiling water and letting them stand for about 3 minutes. Then slip off the skin.

Peanut skins can simply be rubbed off with your fingers. I think they are better with the skins on.

Brazil nuts can be sliced thinly and roasted. They slice more easily if you bring them to boil and simmer them for about 3 minutes in water. Cool slightly and slice.

OVEN METHOD

Spread the nuts on a baking sheet and add 3 tablespoons of butter or nut oil for every pound of nuts. Toast slowly in a preheated 350° F. oven, stirring often, for about 30 minutes, or until roasted. Piñon nuts need no butter or oil. Brazil nuts need only two tablespoons butter or oil.

Salt the nuts with coarse salt and add a little cayenne pepper.

FRYING-PAN METHOD

Use about 4 tablespoons of butter or oil to each pound of nuts and cook slowly over a low flame. Stir continuously until golden brown. Use

2 tablespoons butter or oil to every pound of pine nuts. Brazil nuts are better cooked in the oven.

Salt the nuts in the usual way.

Deviled Almonds

Serve these very hot.

1 **pound almonds**
  Boiling water
2 **tablespoons peanut or vegetable oil**
  Coarse salt
  Cayenne pepper

Skin the almonds by dropping them into boiling water. Dry them.

Heat the oil in a frying pan. Fry the almonds until golden; drain and sprinkle with salt and cayenne pepper.

Stuffed Prunes

Prunes and bacon have a natural affinity for each other. The prunes can be soaked overnight in port after they have been boiled in water, or they simply can be boiled.

24 **prunes, soaked overnight**
24 **almonds or about ¾ cup chutney**
12 **strips of bacon, cut in half**
  Toothpicks

Stone the prunes and stuff the cavity with either almonds or chutney. Wrap the bacon around, secure with a toothpick, and grill until crisp. Makes 24.

Cheddar Cheese with Pistachios

Grate 1 pound white cheddar cheese and beat in enough heavy cream to make a thick paste. Add 1 cup pistachios and shape into a roll. Serve at room temperature on black or pumpernickel bread.

Anchovies with Apples

Serve this either spread on dark bread with drinks before a meal or as a sit-down appetizer with the bread served on the side. It also makes a good addition to a cold buffet table.

Peel, core, and dice 2 crisp eating apples. Drain a tin of anchovies and dice. Fold them into ⅔ cup mayonnaise (preferably homemade). Chill and serve with dark bread.

Cabbage and Apple Salad

Combine 6 chopped celery stalks and half a shredded white cabbage with 2 peeled, cored, and diced eating apples. Mix ¼ cup olive oil with lemon juice to taste, add coarse salt and freshly ground white pepper, and mix.

Beet, Apple, Celery, and Walnut Salad

Combine 2 cooked beets, chopped, 2 chopped apples, 6 chopped celery stalks, and ½ cup chopped walnuts. Mix a dressing of ¼ cup olive or walnut oil with 2 tablespoons vinegar, 2 tablespoons orange juice, coarse salt, and freshly ground pepper. If you like, crush a garlic clove into the dressing and remove it before you pour the dressing on the salad. Mix the dressing with the fruit and vegetables and serve.

Salt Herring with Apples

This Scandinavian dish is good with dark bread as the beginning to a meal or served as a main course for lunch. It also goes well in a cold buffet. Serves 6.

2 salt herring fillets, soaked in water overnight
4 medium boiled potatoes, diced
4 medium beets, cooked and diced
1 pickled gherkin, chopped
2 tablespoons chopped onion
3 crisp apples, unpeeled and diced
   Coarse salt and freshly ground pepper

Dressing
- ½   cup heavy cream
- 1   tablespoon brown sugar
- 2   tablespoons wine vinegar
- 1   teaspoon mustard
  Beet juice
- 2   hard-boiled eggs
  Chopped fresh parsley

Skin and bone herring, after removing the head. Combine it with the other ingredients. Mix the dressing, adding beet juice for color. Chill until ready to serve, pressed down in a mold or large mixing bowl.

To serve, empty upside down out of the bowl. Garnish with quarters of egg and parsley.

Apple and Fig Salad

Since this is a slightly sweet salad, it goes well with ham and pork. It also makes a good contrast to a hot and spicy dish such as curry or chili.

Choose soft, juicy figs and make sure they are not old. If they have been lying around for a long time, they tend to be dry and tough.

- 2   tart apples
- 1   carrot
- 5   dried figs
- 6   dates
- 1   stalk celery

Dressing
  Juice of 1 lemon
- 1   tablespoon ground almonds
- ½   cup heavy cream

Chop the apples (peeled) into small cubes; shred the carrot and put into a salad bowl. Chop up the figs, stone the dates and chop, chop the celery, and add to the bowl. In another bowl mix the lemon juice with the almonds and add the cream, slowly whisking the mixture with a fork. Pour over the salad and toss.

Serves 6.

Cold Asparagus with Walnut Dressing

1	cup finely chopped or blended walnut meats
2	tablespoons vinegar
⅓ to ½	cup walnut or sesame oil
1	tablespoon soy sauce
2	tablespoons sugar
2	pounds cooked asparagus

Mix together the walnuts, vinegar, oil, soy sauce, and sugar. Pour over the asparagus and serve.

Serves 4.

Avocado and Grapefruit Salad

This is good with curries or chili. Slice 2 ripe avocados and a ripe grapefruit, removing the seeds and white pith. You can also slice an orange if you like.

Make a strong vinaigrette sauce with ¼ cup olive oil, 1 teaspoon Dijon mustard, lemon juice to taste, 1 tablespoon vinegar, and 1 garlic clove squeezed into the sauce and removed before serving. Mix well; season with salt and freshly ground white pepper. If you like, serve the salad on oiled lettuce leaves and sprinkle with chives.

Serves 4.

Hazelnut and Bean Salad

1½	cups cooked string beans
1½	cups cooked navy beans
¾	cup roasted hazelnuts (use small ones)

Dressing

6	tablespoons olive oil
2	tablespoons vinegar
1	teaspoon French mustard
	Chopped fresh tarragon (if available)
	Squeeze of lemon
1	clove garlic, crushed in the oil
1	tablespoon shallots, finely chopped
	Coarse salt and freshly ground white pepper

43

Put the beans and nuts into a salad bowl. In a separate bowl mix the dressing and pour it onto the salad, discarding the piece of garlic. Toss gently and serve.

Enough for 4.

Bean Salad with Plum Dressing

For the best results the beans should be warm when the dressing is added. You can use canned beans, but of course cooked dried ones are much better.

This is a very good salad to serve at a buffet. It goes with pork, duck, goose, and fish.

2	cups dried red beans (pinto or kidney)
1	clove garlic
1	fresh chili pepper or ½ teaspoon crushed dried pepper
1	teaspoon fresh basil or ½ teaspoon dried
2	teaspoons fresh coriander or 1 teaspoon dried coriander seed
2 to 3	tablespoons plum jam
1 to 2	tablespoons red wine vinegar
	Freshly ground salt and pepper

Drain the beans and place in large bowl. With a mortar and pestle pound the garlic, pepper, and herbs. Add the jam, pound together, and add the vinegar. Mix well, adding more jam or vinegar according to taste. Season. Pour over the beans and leave overnight, if possible, or a few hours before serving.

Enough for 4.

Cucumbers Stuffed with Cashews

2	cucumbers
¼	cup chopped cashew nuts
2	teaspoons raisins soaked in ¼ cup white wine
2	teaspoons chives, chopped
2	tablespoons cream cheese
	Juice of half a lemon
	Sugar to taste
	Coarse salt and freshly ground black pepper

Peel the cucumbers, cut in half lengthwise, and scoop out the seeds with a teaspoon. Salt them and refrigerate for half an hour. Meanwhile, combine the remaining ingredients, reserving a few of the chives. Dry the cucumbers with paper towels, stuff with the mixture, and sprinkle with chives.

Serves 4.

Orange Salad

The following salads are particularly good with duck, chicken, game, hare or rabbit pâté, pork, and strongly flavored sausage.

For a plain orange salad to serve with duck, peel some oranges, slice very thin, removing the pith and seeds, and sprinkle with kirsch.

Orange and Avocado Salad

1　orange, peeled and sliced, with pith and seeds removed
2　ripe avocados, brushed with lemon juice to keep from turning brown
　　Juice of 1 orange
1　teaspoon finely grated orange peel
1　dried red chili pepper, crushed
　　Finely chopped fresh ginger, if available (small amount)
½　cup raisins soaked in above mixture for an hour
3　tablespoons olive oil
1　tablespoon lemon juice
　　Coarse salt and freshly grated black pepper

Arrange orange in a dish with the avocado slices. Mix raisins and their juice with olive oil and lemon juice. Season with salt and pepper. Pour over the salad; mix and serve.

If you like, this salad can be served on oiled lettuce. A thinly sliced onion and chopped black olives can also be added.

Serves 4.

Orange and Celery Salad

1　orange, peeled, pith and seeds removed, cut into small sections
　　Celery stalks
　　Celery leaves (optional)
3　tablespoons olive oil
1　tablespoon lemon juice
　　Coarse salt and freshly ground black pepper

Combine orange and celery in a bowl and pour on a dressing of the oil and lemon juice. Season with salt and pepper.

Serves 3 to 4.

Orange, Avocado, and Watercress Salad

    Bunch of watercress
2 ripe avocados, sliced
1 orange, peeled and thinly sliced
¼ cup olive oil
2 tablespoons wine vinegar
1 teaspoon Dijon mustard
    Lemon juice
    Coarse salt and freshly ground black pepper
    Pinch of sugar
    Freshly chopped basil, parsley, or chives (optional)

Chop off the stem of the watercress. Arrange cress, avocado, and orange in a salad bowl. Mix a dressing from the olive oil, wine vinegar, mustard, lemon juice, salt, pepper, sugar, and herbs and pour over the salad.

Serves 4.

Orange and Watercress Salad

      Bunch of watercress
1 orange, peeled, pith and seeds removed, cut into small sections
3 to 4 tablespoons sesame or olive oil
1 tablespoon vinegar
¼ teaspoon curry powder
½ teaspoon soy sauce
1 finely chopped shallot (optional)
      Lemon juice
      Coarse salt and freshly ground black pepper

Trim the stems from the cress and combine greens with orange in a salad bowl. Mix the oil, vinegar, curry powder, soy sauce, shallot, and lemon juice (to taste). Season with salt and pepper and pour over the salad.

Dandelion leaves can also be used successfully in this salad.

Serves 3 to 4.

Orange and Olive Salad

1 or 2 oranges, peeled, pith and seeds removed, cut into small sections
Black olives, preferably not canned
Olive oil
Vinegar or lemon juice
Freshly chopped parsley or basil (optional)
Chopped onion
Celery

Mix orange sections with black olives. Pour on a dressing made with 3 parts olive oil to 1 part vinegar or lemon juice. If you like, add a little parsley or basil to the salad. Chopped onion and celery can be added, and the salad can be served with lettuce leaves or watercress.

Serves 4.

Orange and Onion Salad

2 onions
2 oranges, peeled, pith and seeds removed, sliced thinly
Juice of 1 orange
3 tablespoons olive oil
Lemon or lime juice
Freshly chopped marjoram (use dried if fresh is not available)
Coarse salt and freshly ground black pepper

Slice onions and combine in a bowl with the oranges. Mix orange juice with olive oil, lemon or lime juice to taste, marjoram, salt, and pepper. Pour over the salad; toss and serve.

This is particularly good with cold duck or game.

Serves 4.

Orange and Radish Salad

1 to 2 oranges, peeled, pith and seeds removed, cut into quarters and sliced thinly
Bunch of radishes, sliced thinly
Juice of 1 lemon
Coarse salt and freshly ground white pepper
Freshly chopped parsley (optional)

Combine oranges and radishes in a bowl. Squeeze on the juice of a lemon. Season with salt and pepper and sprinkle on parsley if desired.

Serves 3 to 4.

Endive and Orange Salad

This salad goes well with veal, pork, or chicken. While olive oil is a perfectly good oil to use in the dressing, sesame oil is delicious; its delicate nutty flavor goes very well with the endive and oranges.

    4   medium-sized endive
    1   orange
Dressing
    ½   cup orange juice
    1   teaspoon grated orange peel
    3   tablespoons sesame (or olive) oil
    1   garlic clove, crushed
    2   tablespoons soy sauce
        Coarse salt and freshly ground black pepper

Cut off the bottom of the endive and discard the outer leaves. Wipe the other leaves individually and put them in a bowl. Peel the orange and slice thinly, cutting off any white membrane around the outside. Mix the dressing and pour over the salad. Toss and serve.

Enough for 4.

Paprika Salad with Lemon Dressing

This is a good salad to serve with fairly bland veal or pork dishes. It also goes well with turkey.

    2   tart apples
    2   stalks celery
    1   orange
    1   cup halved, shelled walnuts
    1   head Boston lettuce
Dressing
        Juice of half a lemon
    ¼   teaspoon grated lemon peel
    ½   teaspoon dry mustard
    ¾   cup heavy cream
        Coarse salt and paprika (according to taste)

Peel and slice the apples. Chop the celery, peel and chop the orange, and combine in a salad bowl with the walnuts. Wash and dry the lettuce, tear into strips, and add. In another bowl combine all other ingredients except the cream. Little by little beat the cream in. Season and pour over the salad. Toss and serve.

Enough for 4.

Mexican Salad

This is a special salad for festive occasions and is made in Mexico at Christmas time. In fact, it goes well in a buffet dinner or with turkey.

- 2 tangerines
- 1 apple
- 2 bananas
- 3 slices pineapple
- 2 cooked, skinned beet roots
- 1 head Boston lettuce
- 1 green pepper
- 1 red pepper
- ½ cup chopped peanuts
- 1 cup homemade mayonnaise
  Coarse salt and freshly ground black pepper

Peel and section the tangerines. Peel and chop the apple and bananas. Chop the pineapple and beet root and combine all the ingredients in a large salad bowl. Tear the lettuce leaves into medium-sized pieces and add. Chop the peppers and add with the peanuts. Make the mayonnaise, season well, and pour over the salad. Taste, and if necessary add lemon juice. Serve.

Enough for about 8 to 10 people.

Pears with Roquefort Cheese

- 2 fresh pears (peeled)
  Roquefort cheese
- 1 cup homemade mayonnaise
  Boston lettuce
  Parsley

This is one of the few exceptions I make as far as fruit and lettuce combinations served with mayonnaise are concerned. You must use real

Roquefort (blue cheese will not do), and the mayonnaise must be home-made.

Peel and core two fresh eating pears. Fill the centers with Roquefort cheese that is at room temperature. Make 1 cup homemade mayonnaise.

Serve the salad in individual portions on Boston lettuce leaves with mayonnaise spooned over the top. You may toss the lettuce leaves lightly in salad oil if you like. Decorate with a little chopped fresh parsley.

Walnut and Watercress Salad

1   bunch watercress (tough stems cut off)
1   apple, peeled, cored, and diced
2   ounces Gruyère cheese
2   teaspoons chopped Spanish onion
1   cup walnut halves
     Approximately 8 black olives
3   hard-boiled eggs, halved (optional)
½   cup walnut oil°
1   tablespoon red wine vinegar
½   teaspoon Dijon mustard
     Coarse salt and freshly ground black pepper

In a salad bowl combine the cress, apple, cheese, onion, walnut halves, and olives. The eggs can also be added. Make a dressing of the walnut oil with the vinegar, mustard, salt, and pepper. Pour onto the salad, mix well, and serve.

Serves 4.

° Walnut oil has a strange and marvelous flavor. It is delicious on salads. You can buy it in health food stores, but the taste is not so pronounced as that of the French walnut oil. If you can get the French kind, all the better.

Vegetables

Vegetables should be cooked and presented as an important dish in themselves, not as some dreary appendage to meat or fish. A dish of spinach sprinkled with sunflower seeds, artichoke hearts in an orange-flavored sauce and sprinkled with pecans, and red cabbage braised with chestnuts are all dishes that stand on their own. One almost feels like serving them French style, before the meat and not with it. However, vegetables do seem to go with a main course and can complement and enhance a dish. Somehow, pork and prunes or apples are a natural pair; turkey and game go with chestnuts; string beans and almonds go beautifully with delicate chicken or fish dishes.

Fruits and nuts transform plain vegetables into exotic ones. They decorate a table with their color and texture. A plate of yellow fried plantains next to a bowl of black beans served with roast pork; a yellow rice pilaf with dark brown and green nuts, decorated with slices of orange contrasting with dark red slices of pepper; beets in an orange butter with bright green pieces of fresh tarragon sprinkled on top or a white cauliflower covered with a rich dark pumpkin-chili sauce make the table bright and inviting.

Artichoke Hearts with Pecan Sauce Maltaise

Fresh or frozen artichokes are good in this recipe. The sauce can be a little thinner than usual because the pecans will give it body.

    12   fresh artichoke hearts (or 2 packages frozen)
         Sauce Maltaise, page 123
     1   cup chopped pecans
         Chopped fresh parsley to garnish

Cook the artichokes in a very little water. Meanwhile, make the sauce and to it add the pecans. Stir in.

Arrange the hearts on a serving dish (make sure they are very well drained), pour on the sauce, sprinkle with parsley, and serve.

Serves 6.

Nut-Stuffed Artichokes

6	artichokes
1	tablespoon olive oil
1	clove garlic, chopped
1	onion, chopped
½	cup chopped nuts (hazelnuts, almonds, pecans, etc.)
½	cup fresh bread crumbs
1	tablespoon chopped fresh parsley
1	egg
	Lemon juice
1	can anchovy fillets
	Coarse salt and freshly ground pepper
	Boiling water

Trim the stems and cut the sharp points off the leaves of the artichokes with a pair of scissors. Heat the oil in a frying pan and gently cook the garlic and onion until soft. Combine in a bowl with the nuts, bread crumbs, parsley, egg, lemon juice, and salt and pepper. Remove the prickly choke that is in the center of the artichoke between the leaves. Then stuff the mixture into the center of the artichokes. Put them in a fireproof dish, close together so that they retain their shape, and arrange anchovies, chopped, over the top. Pour in water until it reaches ⅓ the way up and bake in a preheated 350° F. oven for 30 to 45 minutes.

Serves 6.

Sautéed Apples

These go with duck, goose, pork, liver, or sausage.

Peel, core, and quarter about 6 cooking apples. Cut the quarters into 3 or 4 slices.

In a large frying pan, heat about 6 tablespoons of butter. Sauté the apples over low heat, turning carefully with a wide spatula when they are golden on one side. Do not let them overcook, or you will end up with applesauce.

If you like, add a little apple brandy or Calvados to the apples and light a match to it to get rid of the harsh alcohol taste. Serve hot.

Serves 4.

Cauliflower with Apples

This is good with roast meat such as pork or veal, sausages, game, and curries.

1　head cauliflower
6　tablespoons butter
6　cooking apples
　　Squeeze of lemon
　　Coarse salt and freshly ground white pepper
　　Nutmeg, freshly grated

Wash the cauliflower and trim away the leaves and any brown bits. Divide into flowerets and cook in a very little boiling water until barely tender (about 3 to 4 minutes). Discard any water, add 3 tablespoons butter, and sauté gently until golden.

Meanwhile, peel, core, and quarter the apples. Cut the quarters into 3 or 4 slices. Heat 3 tablespoons butter in a skillet and gently sauté the apples over low heat until they are golden. Do not stir them or they will break.

Arrange the cauliflower in a serving dish with the apples. Squeeze on some lemon juice, season, and grate a little nutmeg over the vegetables.

Serves 4.

Himmel und Erde

A traditional German dish, the translation means heaven and earth, presumably the potatoes representing earth and the apples heaven. It is a delicious companion to pork, goose, sausages, or duck. In the Rhineland, from which it originates, it is served with blood sausage. Liver sausage goes extremely well, too.

1　pound potatoes
1　pound tart cooking apples
　　Coarse salt and freshly ground pepper
　　Nutmeg, freshly grated

Peel and cube the potatoes; peel, core, and quarter the apples. Cook the potatoes in salted water for about 15 minutes. Drain off most of the water, add the apples and seasonings, and simmer until cooked.

Serves 4.

Fried Bananas

This dish is hardly known outside Latin American or Puerto Rican neighborhoods. I love it and serve it both as a vegetable and as a dessert. (See page 156.) You can use any kind of bananas, but the large green plantains (eaten only when cooked) are best. Simply heat some light oil (peanut, sesame, or vegetable oil) in a frying pan. Cut the bananas in horizontal or vertical slices as you prefer and sauté them until they are lightly browned on each side. Serve hot. Number of servings depends on how many bananas are used.

Banana and Bean Pancakes

This is a Mexican dish and can be a little tricky at first, but it is so good that it is worth trying. The problem is keeping the pancakes together when you fry them. As long as you keep pushing the sides in with a spatula while they are frying, it should work out.

The pancakes are very filling. They go well with pork, chicken, and beef dishes or even as a main course in a vegetarian meal.

6   very ripe bananas
6   tablespoons flour
½   cup melted butter
1   cup peanut or vegetable oil
1   cup refried beans

Mash the bananas well and mix in the flour. Add the butter and mix thoroughly. Heat the oil, and when it begins to smoke, drop in a tablespoon of the mixture. Fry the pancakes, a tablespoon at a time, until they are brown on both sides. Remove and drain on paper towels.

Heat the refried beans and place a teaspoon on each pancake. Fold over and serve very hot.

Enough for 4 to 6.

Note: If you don't want to go to the bother of making your own refried beans (an item that no Mexican kitchen ever seems to be without), you'll find that the canned ones are not bad at all.

String Beans with Almonds

If the beans are young and tender, no liquid should be necessary. If you are using frozen beans, partially thaw them out first and separate them as much as possible.

    1   pound string beans
    1   clove garlic, finely chopped
    1   tablespoon peanut oil
    1   teaspoon finely sliced ginger
    ½   cup slivered almonds
    ¼   cup chicken stock, if necessary
        Coarse salt and freshly ground black pepper

With a vegetable peeler remove the string and ends from the beans and slice them thinly. In a heavy skillet heat the peanut oil. Stir-fry the garlic and ginger. Add the beans and the almonds, salt and pepper and stir-fry until done. If necessary, add a little chicken stock.

Serves 4.

Note: The almonds improve on being put into a hot oven for about 15 minutes before you use them.

Beets in Orange Butter

Use young beets that become available in early summer. Either boil them in their skins (leaving a bit of stem on so that they don't lose their color in the water) or roast them in a slow oven until they are tender. Slip off the skins and toss the beets in the orange butter.

Fresh tarragon is delicious with beets.

    3   ounces butter
    1   tablespoon grated orange peel
    ¼   cup fresh orange juice
        Coarse salt and freshly ground pepper
    1   tablespoon chopped fresh tarragon (or 1 teaspoon dried)
        About 12 small cooked beets

Melt the butter, add the orange peel and juice, seasonings, and tarragon and bring to boil. Add beets, heat through, and serve.

Serves 4.

Broccoli with Hazelnuts

Cauliflower is also good with this sauce.

    1   bunch broccoli
    3   tablespoons butter
    1   tablespoon lemon or orange juice
    ½   cup chopped hazelnuts
        Coarse salt and freshly ground pepper

Trim the broccoli and divide into flowerets. Steam with a very little water.

Melt the butter with the lemon juice, add the hazelnuts, and season. Pour over the drained, cooked broccoli and serve.

Serves 4.

Broccoli Amandine

Prepare the broccoli as for Broccoli with Hazelnuts. Melt half a cup of butter with lemon juice to taste and add ¼ cup chopped toasted almonds. Season and serve over the broccoli.

Serves 4.

Brussels Sprouts with Pecans

Broccoli and cauliflower are also good with this sauce. If you like, add a little orange juice as well as lemon.

    1   pound Brussels sprouts
    2   tablespoons butter
    ½   cup chopped pecans
    2   tablespoons lemon juice
        Marjoram
        Coarse salt and freshly ground black pepper

Cook the Brussels sprouts in very little water. Meanwhile, melt the butter and add the remaining ingredients. Put the sprouts in a heated serving dish and pour on the pecan sauce.

Serves 4.

Chestnuts and Brussels Sprouts

This is very good with pork, turkey, or duck. Cabbage can be substituted for the sprouts.

To peel the chestnuts, make a slit in the side of each one with a sharp knife. Put them in boiling water for a couple of minutes and then turn the heat off. With a slotted spoon take out two or three at a time and peel them while they are still hot. Remove both inner and outer skin. If they cool down, heat them up again because they are impossible to peel while they are cold.

¾ pound fresh chestnuts
1 pound fresh Brussels sprouts
¼ onion, finely chopped
2 strips bacon, chopped
   Water or stock to cover
2 tablespoons butter
1 tablespoon flour
   Coarse salt and freshly ground black pepper
   Freshly ground nutmeg

Peel the chestnuts. Trim the tough outer leaves from the sprouts. Cook the onion and the bacon in 1 tablespoon of the butter. Add the chestnuts and liquid to cover. Simmer gently for 25 to 30 minutes. Meanwhile, using as little water as possible, cook the Brussels sprouts in another pan. When the chestnuts are cooked, add the sprouts. Drain off the cooking liquid and reserve. Melt the remaining butter in a small saucepan, add the flour, and stir for 1 minute without browning. Add the liquid from the chestnuts, bring to boil, and when thickened, pour over the vegetables. Correct seasoning, sprinkle with nutmeg, and serve.

Serves 4.

Stir-Fried Cabbage with Walnuts

1 small head cabbage (Chinese cabbage, if available)
3 tablespoons peanut, sesame, or vegetable oil
1 clove garlic, finely chopped
1 tablespoon fresh ginger, finely chopped (optional)
½ cup chopped walnut meats
   Coarse salt and freshly ground pepper

Shred the cabbage and run under the cold tap to wash it. Drain in a colander.

Heat the oil in a large skillet and fry the garlic with the ginger until golden. Add the cabbage and the walnuts and stir-fry until the cabbage is cooked. It should be bright green and slightly crunchy. Season and serve.

Serves 4 to 6.

Red Cabbage Casserole with Onions and Chestnuts

Red cabbage cooked this way is excellent with roast pork, duck, or goose. The longer you cook it, the better it seems to get, and it is very good reheated.

To peel the chestnuts, see page 135.

1	¼-pound piece of bacon
2	medium-sized onions
2	pounds cabbage, chopped
4	tart apples, peeled and chopped
1	clove garlic
1	bay leaf
	Dash nutmeg, freshly grated
	Coarse salt and freshly ground black pepper
2	cups dry red wine
1	pound peeled chestnuts

Cut the bacon into 1-inch chunks, removing the rind. Fry lightly in a casserole. Chop the onions and fry over low heat without browning for about 5 minutes. Add the chopped cabbage and cook stirring for about 5 minutes so that it is covered with the bacon fat. Add the apples and the remaining ingredients and cook in a moderate oven for about 3 hours. Add the chestnuts and cook for another hour. Remove garlic and bay leaf before serving.

Serves 6 to 8.

Orange-Glazed Carrots

1½	pounds carrots
1	cup stock, bouillon or water
½	cup fresh orange juice
1½	tablespoons sugar
3	ounces butter
4	cloves
	Coarse salt and freshly ground pepper
2	tablespoons chopped fresh parsley

Peel and slice the carrots into 2-inch pieces. Simmer slowly in a covered saucepan with the stock, orange juice, sugar, butter, cloves, and seasonings. When tender and glazed, correct seasoning, scatter parsley on top, and serve.

Serves 6.

Cauliflower with Pumpkin Chili Sauce

1   cauliflower
1   tablespoon peanut or vegetable oil
1   clove garlic, chopped
½   cup pumpkin seeds
¼   cup almonds
    Dash cumin
2   hot chilis, fresh or canned
¾   cup chicken broth
¼   cup chopped fresh coriander or parsley
    Coarse salt and freshly ground pepper

Steam the head of cauliflower intact in a very little water until it is cooked. Meanwhile, prepare the sauce. In a heavy skillet heat the oil. Sauté the garlic, pumpkin seeds, almonds, cumin, and chilis lightly. Purée the mixture in a blender or pound in a mortar. Return to the skillet with the chicken broth. Heat through and simmer gently for about 5 minutes.

Drain the cauliflower. Pour the sauce on, decorate with coriander or parsley, season, and serve.

Enough for 4 to 6.

Eggplant Baked in Coconut Cream

1   large eggplant
2   tablespoons olive oil
3   cloves garlic, chopped
3   tomatoes, sliced
2   onions, sliced
     Coarse salt and freshly ground pepper
     Oregano
     Rosemary
1½   cups coconut cream (see page 130)
2   small red chilis (hot peppers), finely chopped

Slice the eggplant thinly. In a flameproof casserole heat the oil and cook the garlic for 2 minutes. Remove from heat, add slices of eggplant, alter-

59

nating with slices of tomato and onion, finishing with the onion. Season and add herbs as you go. Pour on the coconut cream, sprinkle with chilis, and bake in a preheated 350° F. oven for 45 minutes.

Serves 4.

Eggplant Stuffed with Tomatoes and Pine Nuts

2	eggplants
	Coarse salt
2	tablespoons olive or peanut oil
1	onion, chopped
2	cloves garlic, chopped
¾	pound tomatoes, peeled, seeded, and chopped
	Freshly ground black pepper
	Freshly ground coriander seed
	Dash allspice
4	ounces cooked rice
4	ounces pine nuts
	Lemon juice
2	tablespoons tomato paste
	Water and juice from fresh tomatoes

Remove husks, cut a slice off the stem end of the eggplants, and reserve. With a small knife scoop out the flesh, taking care not to break the skin. Sprinkle the cavity and the flesh with salt and leave for 30 minutes.

Pat the eggplant cavities and flesh dry. Chop up the flesh. Heat the oil in a skillet and soften the onion with the garlic. Add the eggplant flesh, tomatoes, seasonings and spices. Cook until the flesh is soft. Remove and combine in a bowl with the rice, pine nuts, and lemon juice.

Stuff into cavities and seal with the reserved end. Mix the tomato paste with enough water and juice to come ⅓ way up the eggplants, arranged in a baking dish. Bake in a preheated 350° F. oven for 45 minutes to 1 hour.

If you like, you can simmer the eggplants, covered, on top of the stove for 45 minutes.

Serves 4.

Escarole with Olives and Pine Nuts

2 pounds escarole
2 tablespoons olive oil
1 clove garlic, chopped
½ cup black olives, pitted and chopped
¼ cup pine nuts
   Coarse salt and freshly ground black pepper
   Squeeze of lemon juice to taste

Trim off any bad leaves from the escarole. Wash thoroughly.

Heat the olive oil in a deep casserole or frying pan. Fry the garlic until golden but not brown. Add the escarole with the water that still clings to its leaves, the olives and pine nuts. Cover and simmer, stirring occasionally, until cooked (about 10 minutes). Season and serve.

Serves 4 to 6.

Onions Stuffed with Nuts

A tomato or cheese sauce is good with these onions.

4 large onions
   Veal or chicken stock
1 ounce butter
¼ cup chopped nuts (hazelnuts, Brazil nuts, pecans)
¼ cup soft bread crumbs
   Marjoram, thyme, chopped fresh parsley
1 egg
   Coarse salt and freshly ground pepper

Peel the onions, slice off the top, and scoop out the center. Boil in stock to cover for about 20 minutes until nearly soft. Chop up the scooped-out onion and soften in the butter. Mix with the nuts and bread crumbs. Add the herbs and seasonings and bind with a beaten egg. Stuff the onions with the mixture and bake in a preheated 350° F. oven for about 30 minutes, with an inch of stock in the bottom of the pan.

Serves 4.

Spinach with Sunflower Kernels

Any other greens can be used instead of spinach.

- 2 pounds fresh spinach
- 2 tablespoons peanut, sesame, or vegetable oil
- 1 clove garlic, finely chopped (optional)
- 4 tablespoons sunflower kernels
  Coarse salt and freshly ground black pepper

Wash the spinach very carefully in 3 changes of water. Remove any tough stalks. Drain in a colander.

In a large skillet heat the oil. Sauté the garlic and sunflower kernels for about 2 minutes, stirring. Add the spinach, with the water that clings to its leaves, and stir-fry gently until it is cooked. Do not overcook. When the leaves are slightly wilted, it is ready. Season and serve at once.

Serves 6.

Spinach with Peanuts

- 3 tablespoons peanut oil
- 1 clove garlic, chopped (optional)
- 4 tablespoons roasted peanuts
- 2 ounces ham, chopped
- 1 pound spinach, thoroughly washed
  Coarse salt and freshly ground pepper

Heat the oil in a frying pan and fry the garlic until golden. Add the peanuts and ham and fry for 3 minutes. Add the spinach and cook for about 2 minutes so that it is barely wilted and the leaves retain their shape. Season and serve at once.

Serves 4.

Spinach with Sultanas

- 2 pounds spinach
- 2 tablespoons sultanas
- 1 tablespoon butter
- 1 tablespoon olive oil
- 1 clove garlic, chopped
- 1 tablespoon pine nuts
  Coarse salt and freshly ground pepper

Wash the spinach in 3 changes of water and remove any tough stalks. Soak the sultanas in warm water to cover for about 10 minutes.

Heat the butter and oil in a large skillet. Add the garlic, cook without browning for a minute, then add the spinach with the water that clings to its leaves. Cook, stirring constantly, for about 3 minutes. Add the sultanas and pine nuts; cover and cook for another 5 minutes. Season and serve.

Serves 4.

Vegetarian Casserole

Serve this with a mixed or tomato salad and plenty of good bread and cheese.

	Butter
4	cups cooked vermicelli
3	cups milk
6	eggs
3	tablespoons flour
4	pounds spinach (or 4 packages frozen)
3	cups cottage cheese
2	cups sour cream
1	cup ground nuts
10	strips cooked bacon
	Coarse salt and freshly ground black pepper
2	cups grated cheddar cheese
	Paprika

Butter the bottom of a large casserole or baking dish. Put a layer of vermicelli on the bottom. Mix the milk with the eggs and the flour. (Mix the flour to a paste with a little milk first so that it will not be lumpy.) Put a layer of the mixture on the vermicelli. Arrange a layer of washed and dried or thawed chopped spinach over the mixture, add cottage cheese, sour cream, nuts, and bacon, and make layers of alternating ingredients. Season and grate cheddar cheese on the top (the top layer should be the egg mixture) and sprinkle on paprika for decoration. Bake in a 350° F. oven for about 20 to 30 minutes, until brown and bubbling.

Serves 12 to 15.

Glazed Sweet Potatoes with Walnuts

These are good with pork, spareribs, steak, game, turkey, and fried chicken.

6	sweet potatoes
1½	cups brown sugar
3	tablespoons butter
¼	cup brandy
¼	cup water
	Dash nutmeg
½	cup chopped walnuts

Boil the unpeeled sweet potatoes for 15 minutes in water. Drain, cool, peel, and slice. Arrange in a buttered baking dish.

In a small saucepan combine the remaining ingredients except the walnuts. Bring to boil and pour over the potatoes. Add the nuts and bake in a preheated 350° F. oven for 30 minutes, basting occasionally.

Serves 4 to 6.

Tangerine Sweet Potato Casserole

This is very good with roast pork, ham, sausages, or spareribs.

6	sweet potatoes, cooked and peeled
3	tablespoons butter
3	tablespoons brown sugar
	Dash cinnamon
	Squeeze lemon juice
¼	cup dark rum
	Coarse salt and freshly ground black pepper
4	tangerines
3	tablespoons chopped pecans
	Paprika

While the sweet potatoes are warm, mash them with 2 tablespoons butter, brown sugar, cinnamon, lemon juice, rum, and seasonings.

Peel the tangerines, removing the seeds and membrane. Chop and add to the potatoes. Put the mixture in a buttered baking dish and arrange some unpeeled tangerine sections, seeds removed, on top with the pecans. Dot with remaining butter, sprinkle with paprika, and bake in a preheated 350° F. oven for about 20 minutes.

Serves 6.

Zucchini in Yogurt Sesame Sauce

1½ pounds zucchini
2   tablespoons butter
1   tablespoon oil
1   clove garlic, finely chopped
½   cup water
2   tablespoons sesame paste (tahini)
4   tablespoons yogurt
    Freshly grated coriander seed
    Coarse salt and freshly ground white pepper

Slice the zucchini. Heat the butter and oil in a frying pan, add the zucchini, garlic, then the water and cook until the water has dried up and the zucchini are lightly browned. Add the sesame paste, stir well, heat through; add the yogurt and coriander seed and heat through. Season and serve.

Serves 4.

Rice Pilaf with Fruits and Nuts

Leftover chicken, lamb, or pork can be used in this pilaf. Chop the meat and add it to the fruit and nut mixture. Combine it at the end with the cooked rice.

    Peel of an orange
2   tablespoons butter
2   medium-sized onions, chopped
2   tablespoons raisins
1   cup dried apricots, soaked and chopped
1   peach, stoned and chopped
    Inside of the peeled orange, sliced
2   tablespoons chopped almonds
2   tablespoons chopped Brazil nuts
2   tablespoons chopped cashew nuts
    Dash cumin
    Dash mace
¼   cup pistachio nuts
1   bay leaf
    Dash cinnamon
    Coarse salt and freshly ground black pepper
2   cups uncooked long-grain rice
    Pinch of saffron
6   cups water

Blanch the orange peel (drop it into boiling water); drain and dry. Heat the butter in a skillet and cook the onions without browning until clear. Add all the other ingredients except the orange slices, the rice, and the water. Cover and cook over very low heat until the rice is done. Bring water to a boil, add the rice and saffron, and cook over low heat until the water has evaporated. Add the fruit and nut sauce, toss well, and garnish with the orange slices.

Enough for 6 to 8.

Rice with Dates and Almonds

This rice is delicious with stews and curries.

2	cups rice
4	cups water
1	onion, finely chopped
4	tablespoons butter
1	cup blanched almonds, coarsely chopped
2	ounces raisins
½	cup chopped dates
	Coarse salt
½	cup water
	Extra piece of butter

Simmer the rice in the water until cooked.

Meanwhile, soften the onion in the butter. Add the almonds and fry until golden. Add this mixture to the rice and cook until the water has evaporated. Meanwhile, soak raisins in ½ cup water.

Add the fruits and nuts and salt to the rice, mix well, top with the butter, and serve.

Serves 6.

Rice with Pine Nuts, Pistachios, and Almonds

Cook rice as for preceding recipe. Meanwhile, heat 2 tablespoons butter and 1 tablespoon oil in a frying pan. Fry 2 ounces each peeled pistachios, almonds, and pine nuts until golden. Add to the rice, mix in, and top with a piece of butter.

Serves 4 to 6.

Spaghetti with Walnut Sauce*

2 cloves garlic
Olive oil
1 cup walnuts, puréed in a mortar or blender
Boiling water
½ cup finely chopped fresh parsley or basil
1 pound spaghetti
Parmesan cheese, freshly grated

Fry the garlic cloves, chopped, in some olive oil without browning. Add the walnut purée and cook a couple of minutes longer. Remove from the heat and place in a small bowl. Moisten with a little more olive oil and a little boiling water so that it is a thick sauce. Add the parsley or basil.

Meanwhile, cook the spaghetti. When it is done, drain it and mix the sauce thoroughly with the hot spaghetti. Serve with Parmesan cheese.

Serves 3 to 4.

Spaghetti with Pesto*

This is a famous Genoese sauce. You can use parsley instead of basil, but the flavor will be quite different.

Large bunch of fresh basil
1 or 2 cloves garlic
2 tablespoons pine nuts
Coarse salt
2 tablespoons freshly grated Parmesan cheese
Olive oil
1 pound spaghetti
Parmesan cheese to serve with sauce

Put basil in a mortar and chop it with scissors. Chop up the garlic cloves and add. Add pine nuts. Pound in the mortar with a little salt. Add Parmesan cheese and continue pounding until the mixture becomes a thick purée. Then start adding olive oil, little by little, so that the mixture will absorb it. Add about 2 tablespoons altogether. The sauce should be very thick and creamy.

When the spaghetti is cooked, mix the sauce in thoroughly while the spaghetti is still hot. Serve immediately with freshly grated Parmesan cheese.

Serves 3 to 4.

* *Note:* You can keep these sauces covered with a thin layer of olive oil in tightly sealed jars. Refrigerate.

Fish

All over the world people have been inventing new ways of cooking fish and seafood with nuts and fruits, and the most delicious and exotic combinations exist in Latin America and the Middle East. In Mexico's seaports you find dozens of little seafood bars in which, in addition to fresh oysters and beer, you can get crab stuffed with nuts and olives, and fish baked in delicious mixtures of orange and lemon juice, sometimes served in a rich hot red sauce, darkened with a little bitter chocolate. These dishes are nearly always accompanied by fried bananas, rice, and black beans.

In the Middle East, where pomegranates have been eaten since before the Bible was written, subtle and delicate fish dishes are made with pomegranate seeds combined with various nuts and seasonings. Farther east the Chinese have long made delicious meals on shrimp and fish stir-fried and combined with pineapple in a sweet-sour-tasting sauce or sprinkled seafood with roasted sesame seeds, peanuts, or almonds.

The Russians and the Germans are fond of fish cooked with sour cherries, currants, or sultanas. The British favorite in the days of Queen Victoria was mackerel with a sharp gooseberry sauce, while the French cooked sole with grapes and sprinkled slivered almonds over fresh poached trout.

Delicate fish need delicate fruits, whereas the strong fish respond well to sharp sour fruits.

Stir-Fried Shrimp with Walnuts

This Chinese dish is best served over rice. Be very careful not to overcook the shrimp. Shrimp takes only a few minutes to cook, and it keeps on cooking after it has left the stove. It should be firm and juicy, not woolly inside.

2   pounds fresh shrimp
4   tablespoons peanut or vegetable oil
6   slices fresh ginger
1   clove garlic, chopped
1   stalk celery, chopped
1   green pepper, chopped
2   tablespoons soy sauce
2   tablespoons sherry
½   teaspoon cornstarch, mixed to a paste with equal amount of water
½   cup chopped walnuts

Peel the shrimp and set aside. Heat the oil in a large frying pan or *wok* and fry the ginger with the garlic for 1 minute. Add the celery and pepper and fry for 3 minutes, stirring. Then add the shrimp and stir-fry 1 minute. Add the soy sauce, sherry, and cornstarch mixture, bring to boil, and cook until the mixture has thickened. Pour over rice and sprinkle with walnuts.
    Serves 4.

Stuffed Crab Veracruz Style

Fried bananas (page 54), rice, or black beans are the natural accompaniments to this dish.

12   crabs, cooked
 3   tablespoons olive oil
 1   onion, chopped
 2   garlic cloves, chopped
 2   tomatoes, peeled and chopped
½   cup ground almonds
¾   cup chopped pine nuts
 8   pimiento-stuffed olives, thinly sliced
 2   tablespoons chopped capers
     Dash basil or oregano
     Coarse salt and freshly ground black pepper
 3   tablespoons chopped fresh parsley
     About ¾ cup bread crumbs
     Butter
     Paprika

Remove the meat from inside the crabs. Put it into a large bowl. In a frying pan heat the oil and cook the onion with the garlic until soft. Add the tomatoes, cook for about 3 minutes, and then add the remaining ingredients except bread crumbs, butter and paprika. Cook for 5 minutes.

69

Remove and mix with the crabmeat, adding oil if the mixture seems at all dry. Put the stuffed shells into a baking dish, cover with the bread crumbs, dot with butter, and brown under a hot grill. Sprinkle with paprika and a little extra parsley for decoration.

Serves 6.

Shrimp with Pineapple

A Chinese dish; rice goes well with it.

- 2 pounds shrimp
- 1 pound peppers (green, or red and green)
- 2 tablespoons peanut, sesame, or vegetable oil
- 1 tablespoon fresh ginger, sliced
- 1 clove garlic, chopped
- 1 teaspoon sugar
- 2 teaspoons soy sauce
- 1 cup chopped pineapple
- 1 teaspoon dry sherry

Shell and devein the shrimp. Slice the peppers. Heat the oil in a large skillet and fry the peppers with the ginger and garlic. Add the shrimp, stir-fry for 2 minutes, then add remaining ingredients. Cover and cook for about 3 to 5 minutes, until shrimp is cooked. Serve immediately.

Serves 4.

Trout Amandine

Try to get the freshest trout available. Cook them as soon as you have dipped them in the flour—don't leave them in the coating or they will become soggy and the skin will not get crisp.

Serve the trout with plain potatoes and a green vegetable.

- 4 trout, cleaned but with heads on
  Flour
- 4 tablespoons olive oil
- 3 tablespoons butter
- ½ cup slivered almonds
  Lemon wedges
- 2 tablespoons chopped fresh parsley
  Coarse salt and freshly ground black pepper

Wipe the trout, season inside, and dredge with flour that has also been seasoned. Heat the oil until it smokes and put in the fish. Fry until crisp and brown on both sides. Remove to a heated plate. Empty the oil and melt the butter in the pan. Add the almonds and brown. Pour over the trout; garnish with lemon and parsley. Season with salt and pepper.

Serves 4.

Carp with Sultanas

Boiled potatoes sprinkled with dill are good with this Russian dish.

1	2-to-2½-pound carp (or bream)

Court Bouillon

2	carrots
2	stalks celery, plus leaves
1	onion, coarsely chopped
	Bay leaf
	Fresh parsley sprigs
	Thyme
	Peppercorns
	About 2 cups water

1	tablespoon butter
1	tablespoon flour
½	cup white wine
2	tablespoons vinegar
1	teaspoon sugar
1	lemon
½	cup sultanas, soaked in water

Clean the carp. Simmer the ingredients for the *court bouillon* for 20 minutes. Add the carp and poach gently until cooked (about 20 minutes). Strain off 1 cup of the *court bouillon*.

Melt the butter, add the flour, and cook together for 1 or 2 minutes without browning. Add the strained poaching liquid together with the wine and vinegar. Bring to boil, add the sugar, and simmer until reduced. Correct seasoning, add lemon juice to taste and the sultanas, heat through, and pour over the fish. Decorate with parsley and serve.

Serves 4.

Striped Bass with Walnuts

You can serve this fish hot or cold, but you will find that is it better cold. A garlic mayonnaise (homemade, of course) goes very well with it. So would a green mayonnaise.

1   whole striped bass, head on, about 4 pounds
    Coarse salt and freshly ground black pepper
1   onion
2   cloves garlic
    About ½ cup olive oil
1   cup walnuts, finely chopped (or wrap in dish cloth and hammer with a
    rolling pin)
2   green peppers, chopped
1   red pepper, chopped
    About ½ cup chopped fresh parsley
1   cup homemade mayonnaise
    Lemon wedges

Wash and dry the fish. Salt and pepper it inside and out. Chop the onion and mash the garlic. Heat the oil and gently fry the onion and garlic, but do not brown. Add the walnuts and peppers and fry for about 10 minutes over medium-low heat. When the peppers are soft, remove from heat, mix in the parsley and stuff into the fish. Close the cavity with small skewers. Put a couple of tablespoons of oil into a large pan and place the fish in the pan; put into a preheated 400° F. oven. Bake for 30 to 40 minutes, basting continuously. Remove and cool. When lukewarm, pour the mayonnaise over the fish and garnish with lemon wedges. Serve cold.
    Serves 4.

Cod Steaks in Cherry Sauce

Boiled potatoes sprinkled with fresh chopped dill are best with this Russian recipe. You need something to mop up the sauce.

4   codfish steaks
1½   cups milk
½   cup stoned cherries
1   tablespoon butter
2   cloves
     Dash cinnamon
     Dash sugar
½   teaspoon cornstarch
1   glass red wine
     Coarse salt and freshly ground pepper

Cook the codfish steaks in the milk, turning once.

Put the cherries in a small saucepan with just enough water to keep them from sticking. Cook them over low heat and sieve them. Return them to the saucepan with the remaining ingredients, the cornstarch mixed to a smooth paste with a little water. Bring to boil and simmer until thickened. Pour over the well-drained cod and serve.

Serves 4.

Note: I have also made this sauce without sieving the cherries. I suggest you sieve half the cherries and reserve half since I think it makes a more attractive dish with some cherries on top of the fish.

Fried Fish Rolls with Almonds

Rice goes with this Chinese dish. Serve some soy sauce on the table and perhaps a little Chinese mustard if you like.

    3   fish fillets
    3   slices smoked ham
    2   scallions, finely chopped
    1   teaspoon cornstarch
    2   teaspoons soy sauce
    2   teaspoons sherry
    1   teaspoon sugar
    1   egg
    ¾   cup ground almonds
        Peanut or vegetable oil for deep frying
        About 6 slices fresh ginger (if available)

Cut the fish into pieces about 2 × 3 inches. Each fillet should make about 4 pieces. Cut the ham into 1 × 2-inch pieces.

Combine the scallions with the cornstarch, which you have mixed to a paste with the soy sauce, plus the sherry, sugar, and egg. Beat together lightly.

Dip the fish in the mixture and coat one side with almonds. Roll the almond side around the ham and secure with a toothpick.

Heat the oil with the ginger and deep-fry the fish rolls until golden. Drain on paper towels and serve.

Serves 4.

Note: A deep-frying basket is useful here.

Grilled Fish with Walnut Sauce

Use any firm white-fleshed fish for this recipe. The sauce can be made in advance and reheated while the fish is cooking.

A green vegetable such as broccoli, spinach, string beans, or okra would go well with the fish.

4	small or 2 large fish Peanut or sesame oil

Sauce

½	cup walnuts, shelled
1	clove garlic
½	teaspoon Hungarian paprika or cayenne pepper
½	teaspoon fenugreek
½	teaspoon coriander seeds
½	cup finely chopped onion softened in 1 tablespoon peanut or vegetable oil
½ to ¾	cup stock or bouillon made from chicken Freshly ground sea salt and black pepper Freshly chopped parsley

Place the fish on a grill and coat with oil. Set aside.

With a mortar and pestle grind up the remaining ingredients except the stock. Put them in a saucepan with some of the liquid and bring to boil. Add enough liquid so that the sauce is thick and creamy. Season. Meanwhile, grill the fish. When it is cooked, either serve the sauce separately or pour it over the fish. Sprinkle the sauce with chopped fresh parsley before you bring it to the table.

Serves 4.

Note: If it is available, chopped fresh fennel is delicious either in the sauce or cooked with the fish.

Saffron Fish with Pecan Sauce

The saffron makes the sauce a beautiful yellow, and I suggest you serve with this dish contrasting vegetables such as grilled tomatoes, fried zucchini, or a dark green vegetable such as spinach.

To crush the pecans, either grind them with a pestle and mortar or put them in the blender (with the lid on tight!) and blend at high speed for a minute.

4   fish fillets (any boned, skinned white fish except cod or halibut)
1   cup white wine
½   cup fish or chicken broth (or ½ cup wine to 1 cup broth)
1   medium-sized onion
1   clove garlic
3   tablespoons butter
1   teaspoon olive oil
1   cup pulverized pecan nuts
   Dash saffron powder
   Coarse salt and freshly ground black pepper
   Lemon juice
2   tablespoons chopped fresh parsley

Wash and dry the fish. Poach for about 9 minutes in the wine-broth mixture. The fish is done when it is soft but not dry and flaky. Remove to a heated side dish. Chop the onion and mash the garlic. In a skillet heat the butter and the oil. Add the onions and garlic and cook until the onions are clear, without browning. Add the pecan nuts, the saffron powder, salt and pepper and stir. Add the fish poaching liquid and boil down until thick. Season with lemon juice to taste. Pour over fish, decorate with chopped parsley, and serve.

Serves 4.

Note: A tablespoon of chopped fresh ginger added to the pan with the onion and garlic is delicious.

Poached Fish in Almond-Tomato Sauce

This sauce is rich and dark. The best way to serve the fish is over rice, in its sauce, with fresh coriander or parsley chopped and scattered over the top.

⅓   cup olive oil
1   clove garlic, chopped
2   onions, chopped
1   small can tomatoes, plus juice
1   cup white wine
   Bay leaf
   Dash basil
   Coarse salt and freshly ground pepper
1   cup blanched almonds
3   pounds fresh nonfat white fish
1   tablespoon grated bitter chocolate
   Chopped fresh coriander or parsley

Heat the oil in a heavy large skillet. Sauté the garlic with the onion until softened. Add the tomatoes, wine, bay leaf, and basil. Season and simmer, covered, for 45 minutes.

Meanwhile, pound the almonds in a mortar or in the blender. Combine with the sauce. Add the fish and poach for about 10 to 12 minutes, or until it flakes when tested with a fork. Add the chocolate, correct seasoning, heat through, scatter on the coriander, and serve.

Serves 4 to 6.

Baked Fish with Pomegranate Seed and Walnut Stuffing

Serve this with Tahini Paste, page 126, thinned down with a little water. Rice goes well with it.

1	3½-to 4-pound fish (any firm whole white fish)
1	cup olive oil
	Juice 1 lemon
	Coarse salt
2	medium onions, finely chopped
3	green peppers, finely chopped
1	cup finely chopped walnuts
½	cup chopped fresh parsley
4	tablespoons fresh pomegranate seeds
	Freshly ground pepper
	Tahini paste
1	lemon, sliced
	Paprika

Dry the fish thoroughly and place in a baking dish into which you have poured about ¼ cup of the olive oil. Squeeze the lemon juice inside and outside the fish. Season with salt and another ¼ cup oil.

Heat the remaining oil in a frying pan and soften the onion with the peppers without browning. Add the walnuts and fry for 3 minutes. Remove and stir in the parsley, pomegranate seeds, and seasonings. Stuff into the fish and close the cavity with skewers.

Bake for 40 minutes, or until done, in a preheated 450° F. oven, basting frequently.

Pour on the tahini paste, arrange lemon slices on top, and garnish with parsley and paprika.

Serves 4 to 6.

Baked Mackerel with Pine Nut Stuffing

    4   small mackerel, cleaned
    ¼   cup olive oil
    1   onion, finely chopped
    ½   cup chopped pine nuts
    1   cup white bread crumbs
        Freshly ground coriander seeds
    2   ounces currants
        Coarse salt and freshly ground white pepper
        Chopped fresh parsley to garnish
    1   cup *court bouillon*

Wipe the mackerel with paper towels and set aside. Heat the oil in a frying pan and soften the onion. Add the pine nuts, bread crumbs, coriander, currants, and seasonings. Fry for 5 minutes. Remove and stuff into the mackerel cavity, securing with a skewer.

Put in a baking dish, add the *court bouillon,* and bake for 20 to 25 minutes in a preheated 450° F. oven. Sprinkle with parsley.

Serves 4.

Note: Court bouillon is made by boiling water with a bay leaf, peppercorns, thyme, parsley, and chopped onion and carrot. Simmer 30 minutes and strain.

Mackerel with Gooseberry Sauce

This is a Victorian dish and is very popular in England. In France gooseberries are called *groseilles à maquereau,* meaning mackerel gooseberries, whereas *groseilles* alone means red currants.

The mackerel may also be poached in a *court bouillon* instead of grilled and the sauce served in the same way, but use the poaching liquid instead of the water in the sauce.

    2   large or 4 small mackerel
        Fresh fennel, if available
Sauce
    1   pound gooseberries
    3   ounces sugar
    2   ounces butter
    2   teaspoons flour
    ¼   pint water or white wine
        Coarse salt and freshly ground white pepper
        Nutmeg or ground ginger

Score the mackerel, season, and place some fennel inside. Grill, turning once only, under the broiler. Meanwhile, make the sauce.

Boil the gooseberries with the sugar in water to cover until tender. Sieve.

Melt the butter in the saucepan. Add the flour and, stirring, cook for a minute. Meanwhile, bring the water or wine to the boil. Add all at once to the butter-flour mixture, stirring vigorously. Season, and cook until thickened. Add the gooseberries, cook together to heat through, taste for seasoning, and add nutmeg or ginger as you wish.

Serves 4.

Red Snapper with Almond Sauce

Serve this with a green vegetable. If you cannot get red snapper, any firm white non-oily fish will do.

1	2- to 3-pound red snapper (or 2 smaller ones)
	Coarse salt and freshly ground pepper
	Olive oil

Almond Sauce

1	cup finely chopped or ground almonds
3	hard-boiled eggs
3	tablespoons dark mustard
	Squeeze of lemon or lime juice
3 to 4	tablespoons olive oil
2	tablespoons chopped fresh parsley
	Some pimiento slices (optional)
	Some lemon quarters

Clean the snapper, season the cavity, and put it into a greased baking dish with a little oil on top. Bake in a preheated 350° F. oven until done.

Meanwhile, make the sauce. Put the almonds into a mixing bowl. Add the yolks of the eggs, mustard, lemon, oil, and parsley. Mix well and season. It should be a smooth paste. Add the chopped egg whites.

Remove fish to a heated serving dish. Pour on the sauce, garnish with pimiento and lemon quarters, and serve.

Enough for 4.

Red Snapper Yucatan Style

Serve this Mexican dish with rice or fried bananas (page 54).

- 1   4- to 5-pound red snapper (or 2 small fish)
- 1   lemon or lime
    Coarse salt and freshly ground white pepper
- ¼   cup olive oil
- 1   onion, chopped
- ½   cup green olives
- ½   pimiento, sliced
- 1   teaspoon ground annatto seeds
- 2   large oranges
- 2   tablespoons chopped fresh coriander or parsley
- 2   hard-boiled eggs

Marinate the fish in the lemon juice for about half an hour. Season and put into a well-buttered baking dish.

Heat the oil in a skillet and soften the onion without browning. Add the olives, pimiento, and annatto seeds, pulverized in a blender or with a pestle and mortar. Add the juice of the oranges. Cook over moderate heat for about 3 minutes. Pour the sauce on the fish, scatter on the coriander or parsley, and bake in a preheated 400° F. oven for about 30 minutes or until the fish flakes when tested with a fork.

Garnish with chopped hard-boiled eggs and fresh coriander.

Serves 4.

Poached Sole Veronique

Use seedless white grapes for this recipe. Serve potatoes with the fish and a salad afterward.

- 4   sole, skinned and boned
- 4   shallots, chopped
- 1   cup white wine
- ½   cup fish stock or chicken broth
    Coarse salt and freshly ground black pepper
- 3   tablespoons butter
- 1½   tablespoons flour
- 1   cup heavy cream
    Lemon juice
- 1   cup white seedless grapes
    Boiling water
- 1   tablespoon butter (for grapes)

Wash and dry the sole. Put the fish and shallots in a shallow pan and cover with the wine and fish stock. Season, and simmer very gently for about 9 minutes, depending on the size of the fish. It is done when the flesh is soft and pierces easily. Don't overcook. Remove the fish to a heated side dish.

Boil down the wine and stock. In a medium-sized saucepan melt the butter. Add the flour and stir together, without browning, for about 1 minute. Add the boiling liquid all at once and stir over the heat for a further minute or until it seems to be about the right consistency (like thick cream). Add the cream slowly over the heat, stirring all the time. Remove from heat and correct seasoning; add lemon juice to taste.

Drop the grapes into boiling water for a couple of minutes. Remove and drain. Heat the butter and sauté the grapes for a couple of minutes. Spoon the sauce over the fish, decorate with the grapes, and serve immediately.

Serves 4.

Sole with Bananas

    8   fillets of sole
    ¼   pound melted butter
        About 2 cups fresh fine bread crumbs
        Coarse salt
        Cumin
    4   bananas
        Juice 1 lemon
    1   teaspoon finely chopped lemon rind
        Chopped fresh parsley to garnish

Dip the fillets first into the butter and then into the bread crumbs. Season, sprinkle with melted butter, and grill until golden brown.

Meanwhile, fry the bananas, peeled and cut in half lengthwise, in butter. Arrange the fish on a serving dish. Put the bananas on top; sprinkle with lemon juice and the rind. Scatter on the parsley and serve.

Serves 4.

Poultry

Of all the meats in the United States, perhaps the most responsive to cooking in strongly flavored sauces is the American chicken. Commercial production has rendered the meat bland and virtually tasteless, but chicken is transformed when it is marinated in fruit juices, cooked with lemons, oranges, prunes, or kumquats, and served with a spicy nut sauce.

In Latin America chicken is often steamed in fruit juice, which makes it tender and gives it a delicious flavor. Spices and chili are often added, and color as well as taste plays an important part. The native turkey is cooked in a strong dark chocolate-chili sauce with a variety of fruits and nuts or stuffed with bananas, nuts, and other fruits. Farther north the bird takes on a more familiar aspect when it is stuffed with sausage meat and chestnuts and served with a cranberry sauce.

In the Middle East poultry is the usual festive dish, and special care is taken in cooking the bird. There is an extraordinary variety of ways to prepare poultry whether it is served under a sauce of crushed hazelnuts or pistachios, poppy seeds, pomegranate seeds, or rose hips, or cooked with rhubarb, quinces, or in a strange delicate sauce made with pistachios and perfumed with rose water. These dishes go back hundreds of years. Today one still finds luscious fruit and chicken dishes in Morocco; Turkish and Syrian dishes using walnuts and hazelnuts; and the lemon and garlic sauces of Egypt.

Farther east the Chinese discovered the haunting flavor of tangerine peel cooked with duck; cashews and kumquats were used in sauces, as were lichee fruits, almonds, and red dates. In India coconut milk often forms the base of a curry, and walnuts, pistachios, and pomegranate seeds are as popular as in the Middle East.

French dishes such as chicken with grapes and duck with cherries or oranges have become classics in the West, and game is traditionally served with the strong flavors of chestnuts, gooseberries, oranges, and cranberries.

Chicken Breasts with Pistachio Nuts

Use unsalted green pistachios for this recipe. Do not use the kind with the red dye. Rice is the best accompaniment.

4   chicken breasts
2   tablespoons butter
4   shallots, finely chopped
¼   pound mushrooms, sliced
⅓   cup dry white wine
2   egg yolks
⅓   cup heavy cream
⅓   cup chopped pistachio nuts
1   tablespoon chopped tarragon (fresh if available)
    Lemon juice
    Coarse salt and freshly ground white pepper

Wipe the chicken breasts dry with paper towels. Heat the butter in a heavy skillet and brown the breasts without burning. Add the shallots and cook until softened. Add the mushrooms, cook for a minute, and then add the wine. Cover and cook for about 15 minutes.

Beat the egg yolks into the cream. Add the hot sauce from the chickens and mix well. Put the chicken breasts on a warm serving dish and keep hot. Return the sauce to the skillet and add the pistachio nuts, tarragon, lemon juice, and seasonings. Heat through gently until thick. Do not boil. Correct seasoning and pour over the chicken.

Serves 4.

Chicken Veronique

4   chicken breasts
    Fresh tarragon if available
    Coarse salt and freshly ground white pepper
2   tablespoons butter
1   onion, chopped
½   cup chicken stock
½   cup white wine
2   cups seedless grapes
¼   cup thick cream

Dry the chicken breasts and put pieces of tarragon under the skin. If you cannot get fresh tarragon, use dried in the sauce but don't put it under the skin. Season the chicken pieces and brown in the butter.

Remove to a side dish. Soften the onion in the butter and place the chicken in a casserole with the stock and wine. Bring to boil and bake in a preheated 350° F. oven for 20 to 30 minutes.

Remove chicken to a serving dish. Bring sauce to boil, add grapes and cream, heat through, correct seasoning, and pour over the chicken. Sprinkle on some chopped fresh tarragon if you like.

Serves 4.

Chicken with Fruits and Nuts

Serve this with rice and a green vegetable. The chicken improves if marinated in the juice overnight.

1	frying chicken, cut up
	Juice of 3 oranges and 1 lemon
2	tablespoons olive oil
2	onions, chopped
2	garlic cloves, chopped
4	tomatoes, chopped
1	tablespoon chopped capers
3	tablespoons raisins
6	prunes, stoned and chopped
¼	pound chopped ham
½	cup ground or finely chopped almonds
2	cloves
1	stick cinnamon
	Dash nutmeg
2	tablespoons wine vinegar
	Coarse salt and freshly ground pepper

Marinate the chicken in the orange and lemon juice for at least 2 hours, preferably overnight.

Pat the chicken dry with paper towels, reserving the marinade. In a heavy skillet or casserole heat the oil and brown the chicken lightly. Remove to a side dish. Add the onion and the garlic and cook without browning until onion is soft. Add the tomatoes, cook for about 3 minutes, then return the chicken to the pan with its marinating juices and add the remaining ingredients. Simmer over low heat until chicken is cooked (about half an hour).

Enough for 4.

Casserole Chicken with Kumquats

Serve plain rice with this chicken dish. Because of its oriental character a vegetable such as snow peas or Chinese cabbage would go well with it.

1   chicken, about 3 pounds
1   tablespoon peanut oil
2   tablespoons butter
4   scallions, chopped
1   clove garlic, mashed
1   tablespoon finely chopped fresh ginger (if available)
1   cup fresh orange juice
    Juice of half a lemon
2   tablespoons soy sauce
    About 10 kumquats cut in halves
    Coarse salt and freshly ground black pepper
    Lemon slices to garnish

Wash the chicken and cut it up into frying pieces. Dry it thoroughly. In a casserole heat the oil and the butter. Sauté the chicken pieces until they are lightly browned on all sides. Remove to heated side dish. Add the scallions, garlic, and ginger and fry gently for about 3 minutes. Add the orange and lemon juice and the soy sauce and scrape up all the bits sticking to the bottom of the casserole. Return the chicken to the casserole with the kumquats. Season and simmer slowly, uncovered, in the upper third of a preheated 375° F. oven for about 30 minutes or until the juices run clear and yellow when the chicken is pricked with a fork. Garnish with lemon slices and serve.

Serves 4.

Chicken in Sesame-Coconut Sauce

Sesame-coconut butter can be bought in any health food store. It keeps well and can be used in a variety of dishes.

1   3- to 4-pound chicken, cut up
2   tablespoons peanut, sesame, or vegetable oil
2   cloves garlic, finely chopped
2   hot chilis, chopped (fresh or canned)
1   teaspoon chili powder
1 to 2 cups chicken broth (or more if necessary)
3   tablespoons sesame-coconut butter
        Coarse salt and freshly ground pepper
        Chopped fresh parsley to garnish

Dry the chicken with paper towels. Heat the oil in a large heavy fireproof casserole. Brown the chicken pieces. Remove to a side dish.

Add the garlic to the casserole and cook until golden. Add the chilis and chili powder, cook for a minute, and add the chicken broth and sesame-coconut butter. Mix well, return the chicken to the pan, season, and simmer until cooked (about 30 minutes). Garnish with parsley and serve.

Serves 4.

Tarragon Chicken with Peaches

This is a superb summer dish for people lucky enough to get both fresh tarragon and peaches. Serve it with Rice with Dates and Almonds, page 66.

1	frying chicken, cut up
	Fresh tarragon
	Lemon or lime juice
1	tablespoon oil
4	tablespoons butter
1	onion, chopped
	Coarse salt and freshly ground white pepper
½	teaspoon turmeric
1½	cups stock (or more to cover)
6	fresh peaches
	Paprika

Put pieces of fresh tarragon under the skin of the chicken. Squeeze with the lemon juice and leave for 1 to 2 hours.

Heat the oil and 2 tablespoons butter and brown the chicken. Remove and lower heat to soften the onion in the butter and add salt, pepper and turmeric. Return the chicken to the casserole and add the stock. Simmer gently for about 20 minutes.

Meanwhile, stone the peaches and cut them in slices. Toss them in the remaining butter.

If there seems to be too much liquid in the chicken, drain it off and boil it down. Return it to the chicken and arrange the peaches on top. Simmer until the chicken is done (another 15 to 20 minutes). Correct seasoning and sprinkle with paprika and extra tarragon.

Serves 4 to 6.

Chicken with Prunes

Rice and squash are good accompaniments for this dish. You can either simmer the chicken on top of the stove or bake it in the upper third of a preheated 375° F. oven.

1	chicken, about 3 pounds
2	tablespoons olive oil
1	tablespoon butter
1	onion, chopped
1	clove garlic, mashed
2	green peppers, chopped
1	red pepper, chopped
2	tomatoes, chopped and skins removed by dropping the tomatoes into boiling water for a minute
½	pound prunes soaked overnight in water and pitted
	Dash cinnamon
	Dash thyme
	Dash rosemary
	Coarse salt and freshly ground black pepper
3¼	cups red wine
	Water from the prunes to cover

Wash the chicken and cut it up into frying pieces. Dry thoroughly on paper towels. In a casserole heat the oil and the butter. Add the onion and garlic and cook slowly until the onion is clear but not browned. Add the peppers and cook for about 3 minutes. Add the tomatoes and the prunes and cook for 5 minutes. Add the spices and herbs, the seasonings, and the chicken. Add the wine and the prune juice to cover the chicken. Cover and simmer for about 45 minutes to an hour or until the juices of the chicken run clear and yellow when pierced by a fork.

Serves 4.

Chicken Saté with Peanuts

These are Indonesian kebabs. You need small wooden skewers for the chicken. This is a very good dish cooked outside on a barbecue grill. If this is not possible, broil them. Rice goes best with the chicken.

1 3½-pound chicken
Coarse salt and freshly ground pepper
1 clove garlic (optional)
⅔ cup coconut cream (page 130)

Sauce
1 tablespoon peanut oil
1 cup peanuts, pulverized in a blender or with pestle and mortar
1 teaspoon chili powder
1 teaspoon grated lemon rind
1½ teaspoons brown sugar
1 cup chicken stock
Juice of half a lemon

Cut the chicken into 1-inch pieces, removing the bones. Season and marinate with the garlic, crushed, in the coconut cream. Leave for 6 hours or overnight.

Heat the oil in a saucepan and toss the peanuts until golden. Add the remaining ingredients except lemon juice and simmer, covered, for 20 minutes. Add the lemon juice, correct seasoning, and serve with the kebabs.

Drain off the marinade and thread the chicken pieces on skewers. Brush with a little oil and broil, basting occasionally with the marinade.

Serves 6.

Chicken with Pine Nut Sauce

Serve this with rice decorated with chopped red pimiento and a green vegetable.

2 2-pound chickens, cut up
5 tablespoons peanut or sesame oil
1 onion, sliced
1 carrot, sliced
1 stalk celery plus leaves, chopped
Herb bouquet (parsley, bay leaf, thyme tied in cheesecloth)
1 cup white wine
Water
½ cup pine nuts
Dash sugar
Dash cinnamon
Coarse salt and freshly ground pepper
2 eggs
Lemon juice
¼ cup dry sherry
2 tablespoons chopped fresh parsley or coriander

Dry the chicken pieces well; heat 3 tablespoons of the oil in a deep pan and brown them. Remove. Turn down the heat and soften the vegetables. Add the herbs, wine, chicken, and water to cover. Simmer gently for about 40 minutes.

Meanwhile, pulverize the pine nuts with a pestle and mortar. In another pan heat the remaining oil and brown the pine nuts. Add 1½ cups of the chicken broth and seasonings and simmer gently for 10 minutes. Beat the eggs and off heat gradually add the sauce, beating continuously. Return to saucepan over low heat, heat through until thick, squeeze in some lemon juice, add the sherry, and pour over chicken pieces. Decorate with parsley or coriander and serve.

Enough for 4 to 6.

Chicken with Curried Cashew Sauce

1	chicken
3	carrots
1	onion
2	stalks celery, with leaves
	Bay leaf
1	tablespoon chopped fresh parsley
	Coarse salt
	Water to cover

Curried Cashew Sauce

3	tablespoons cashew nuts
1½	tablespoons butter
1	onion, chopped
1	apple, chopped
1	pound potatoes, peeled and diced
2	tablespoons mild curry paste
1½	cups milk
1½	cups chicken stock (from boiled chicken)
2	tablespoons raisins
	Lemon juice to taste
	Coarse salt and freshly ground pepper
¼	cup thick cream

Simmer the chicken with the vegetables and spices in water to cover for about 1½ hours. Cool it in its broth.

Fry the nuts in the butter until golden. Add the onion, fry until soft, then add the apple and potatoes. Stir in the curry paste, milk, and stock.

88

Add the raisins and remaining sauce ingredients. Simmer for 30 minutes or until the potatoes are cooked.

When ready, add the chicken, cut in pieces, and heat through. Serve with rice.

Serves 4.

Pollo Pibil (*Chicken Steamed in Fruit Juice*)

Rice is a good accompaniment to this Latin American dish.

1   3- to 4-pound chicken, cut up
1   cup fresh orange juice
½   cup fresh lime or lemon juice
1   clove garlic, finely chopped
1   tablespoon annatto seeds, ground in blender or pulverized in mortar
1   teaspoon dried cumin seeds, pulverized in mortar
    Oregano
    Ground cloves
    Cinnamon
    Coarse salt and freshly ground pepper

Put the chicken in a baking dish. Combine the remaining ingredients and pour over the chicken. Marinate overnight or for at least 6 hours.

Put two large sheets of aluminum foil in a colander and arrange the chicken on it, making sure that it is leakproof. Pour in the marinade, then pull together the foil and twist it so that no air will get into the chicken.

Put the colander in a large saucepan or pot and pour in enough water to come to within an inch of the bottom of the colander. Bring to boil, cover, and let simmer for about 2 hours or until the chicken is cooked. Add more water if necessary.

Serves 4.

Aji de Gallina

This is a Peruvian dish. It is delicious and tremendously filling, so I would advise nothing more than a salad to go with it. It is a good party dish since it looks attractive and can be made in advance and heated through.

1   4-pound chicken, cut up
    Cold water to cover
3   onions, chopped
2   carrots, chopped
1   stalk celery, chopped
8   slices fresh homemade-style white bread, crusts off
2   cups milk
⅔   cup olive oil
1   garlic clove, chopped
1   tablespoon annatto seeds, pulverized in a mortar or blender
2   tablespoons dried red chilis, pulverized in a mortar or blender
1   cup walnuts, pulverized in a mortar or blender
    Coarse salt and freshly ground black pepper
⅓   cup freshly grated Parmesan cheese
3   hard-boiled eggs, quartered
12 black olives
2   fresh hot chilis or pimiento, cut in strips

Simmer the chicken in the water with 1 onion, carrots, and celery for about 20 to 30 minutes, until cooked. Drain and reserve stock for another use. Skin, bone and slice the chicken into thin strips.

Soak the bread in one cup of the milk for 5 minutes. With your hands mash the bread and milk together to make a thick paste.

Heat the oil in a large heavy skillet. Soften the remaining onions with the garlic and cook for 5 minutes. Add the annatto, chilis, walnuts, and seasonings. Reduce heat and simmer 5 minutes. Add the bread paste and the remaining cup of milk. Simmer, stirring constantly, until the sauce thickens. Add the chicken and the cheese and heat through.

To serve, put the chicken mixture into a large fairly deep dish and arrange the eggs, olives, and chilis in a spokelike pattern on top.

Serves 4 to 6.

Duck with Pear and Chestnuts

1   3- to 4-pound duck
3   tablespoons peanut oil
1   cup good stock
3   tablespoons sherry
2   tablespoons soy sauce
3   slices ginger
½   pound chestnuts, peeled (page 135)
1   large pear
2   teaspoons sugar

Chop the duck into 2-inch chunks (including the bones). Heat the oil in a skillet and fry the duck until browned. Drain off the fat and return the duck to the pan with the stock, sherry, soy sauce, and ginger. Cover and simmer for 30 minutes.

Add the chestnuts and simmer for 10 to 15 minutes.

Peel and core the pear. Slice and sprinkle with sugar. Add to the pan and cook for about 5 minutes.

Serves 4.

Roast Duck with Cherries

Duck with cherries is known as Canard Montmorency in France where this dish originates. Since the French like their duck medium rare, I have given those cooking times. If you like yours more well done, add on a little time, but remember that overcooked duck is dry and disappointing.

1	4- to 5-pound duck
	Coarse salt and freshly ground pepper
2	tablespoons butter
	Dash of thyme, sage, and parsley
⅔	cup Madeira or red wine
1	cup meat stock or stock made from duck giblets, etc.
½	pound cherries, stoned
1	small glass cherry liqueur, port, or cognac
1	teaspoon sugar to taste, if necessary

Season the cavity of the duck and put the butter inside. Sprinkle in some herbs. Roast the duck in a preheated 350° F. oven for about 1 hour and 30 minutes. The juices should run pinkish yellow.

Deglaze the roasting juices with the wine or Madeira, having poured off as much fat as possible. Add the stock and bring to boil. Simmer for about 5 minutes and strain. Add to the cherries in a small saucepan and heat, below simmering, for about 5 minutes. If you boil the liquid, the cherries may shrivel. Add the liqueur, and sugar if they are morello cherries.

Remove the cherries and arrange them around the duck on a serving dish. Boil up the sauce to thicken it and stir in a tablespoon of softened butter. Pour some around the duck and serve the rest in a sauce boat.

Serves 4.

Canard à l'Orange

This is the best-known way of cooking duck. The bird is garnished with fresh orange slices and watercress and is accompanied by a rich orange-flavored brown sauce. The sauce must be prepared before the duck has finished cooking.

1   4- to 5-pound duck
     Coarse salt and freshly ground pepper
5   oranges

Giblet Stock

2   cups water
1   onion, stuck with cloves
1   carrot, coarsely chopped
     Bay leaf, thyme, sage, parsley

Sauce

2   tablespoons sugar
2   tablespoons vinegar
2   tablespoons arrowroot mixed with 2 tablespoons stock
½   cup port or Madeira
1   tablespoon red currant jelly (optional)
2   tablespoons orange liqueur
     Lemon juice to taste
1   bunch watercress to garnish

Clean the duck and prick all over with a fork so that the fat will escape during cooking. Peel and slice one orange, reserving the peel. Season the cavity and place the orange inside.

Roast the duck in a preheated 350° F. oven for 1½ hours, turning it occasionally.

Meanwhile, make the stock. Simmer the giblets with the onion, carrot, herbs, and seasonings in the water for 30 minutes.

Cut the orange peel into very thin strips (*julienne*) and simmer 15 minutes in water to cover. Drain and set aside.

Bring the sugar and vinegar to boil in a small saucepan until brown. Do not burn. Add the strained duck stock and simmer for 2 minutes, stirring. Add the blended arrowroot and the orange peel. Simmer for 4 minutes until the sauce has thickened. Correct seasoning and set aside.

Peel and slice the remaining oranges.

When the duck is cooked, put it on a heated plate. Keep warm in the oven with the door open.

Pour the duck fat from the roasting pan and scrape up the cooking juices with the port. Strain into the sauce. Add the orange liqueur. Bring to boil, correct seasoning, and add lemon juice to taste. Pour into a sauce boat.

Arrange the orange slices over the duck and garnish with watercress. Serves 4.

Casserole Roasted Duck with Pineapple

1	4- to 5-pound duck
2	tablespoons butter
1	tablespoon oil
¾	cup rum
¾	cup pineapple juice
6	slices pineapple (preferably fresh)

Duck Giblet Stock

	Duck giblets
1½	cups water
1	onion
1	carrot
1	stalk celery plus leaves
	Thyme, bay leaf
	Coarse salt and freshly ground pepper
1	tablespoon arrowroot

Wipe the duck inside and out and season the cavity. Prick the skin with a fork and brown the duck in the butter and oil, drain off the fat, and boil up the rum with the pineapple juice.

In a heavy casserole place the duck with the rum-pineapple juice and arrange the pineapple slices on top. Roast, covered, in a preheated 325° F. oven for about 1½ hours.

Meanwhile, simmer the duck giblets in the water with the vegetables and seasonings.

When the duck is cooked, remove it to a heated serving dish. Drain off the fat and bring to boil, scraping up any coagulated cooking juices. Add the stock and remaining pineapple juice and rum. Mix the arrowroot with a little water and add. Correct seasoning and when thickened serve separately in a sauce boat.

Serves 4.

Simmered Duck with Tangerine Peel

Rice and Duk Sauce, page 122, goes with this dish. If you wish to save the stock for use in other dishes, refrigerate it, and when you are ready to use it, remove the fat in one big lump when it is cold and congealed.

1   3- to 4-pound duck
    Water to cover
2   ounces tangerine peel, chopped
5   slices fresh ginger
3   scallions, chopped
    Coarse salt and freshly ground pepper

Wipe the duck and place in a heavy saucepan with water to cover. Add the remaining ingredients and simmer for 1½ hours.
Serves 4.

Goose with Gooseberry Sauce

Potatoes roasted in the pan with the goose would go well here.

The amount of sugar you need in the sauce will vary according to how sour the gooseberries are.

1   8- to 10-pound goose
1   tablespoon dried sage
2   tablespoons crushed juniper berries
    Coarse salt and freshly ground pepper
1   small onion, coarsely cut
Sauce
¾   pound gooseberries
    About 3 tablespoons sugar
½   cup chicken stock
½   cup white wine

Prick the skin of the goose so that the fat will escape when it cooks. Inside the cavity put the sage and some of the juniper berries, spreading the rest over the goose. Season the cavity and put in the onion. Roast in a 400° F. oven for about 20 minutes, then turn the oven low to about 300° F. for about 3 hours so that it will cook slowly and come out juicy and tender without being too fatty. Meanwhile, cook the gooseberries with the sugar, stock, and wine. Correct sweetness and serve separately with the goose.
Enough for 6.

Roast Goose with Apples and Prunes

In Scandinavia this is the traditional Christmas bird, and in Denmark it is served on Christmas Eve. The Scandinavian way of stuffing it with prunes and apples is one of the best since it cuts the fat, and the bird comes out less greasy.

Serve red cabbage (see page 58 for Red Cabbage with Chestnuts) and potatoes with the goose.

Don't buy a goose heavier than 10 pounds, or it will be tough.

1	9- to 10-pound goose
1	lemon
20	prunes soaked overnight in red wine or water
6	cooking apples, peeled, cored, and quartered
½	pint boiling stock made from the giblets simmered in water with onion, carrot, etc.
1	tablespoon flour
	Coarse salt and freshly ground black pepper
	Caraway seeds (optional)
	Marjoram (optional)

Clean the goose and remove the excess fat. Stone the prunes. Rub the goose inside and out with the lemon, salt, and pepper. Stuff the cavity with the prunes and apples. Truss and sew up. Prick the skin all over with the prongs of a fork to allow the fat to escape while roasting.

In a preheated 350° F. oven roast the goose for about 2½ hours, basting occasionally. If the goose has a lot of fat, pour it off several times during roasting. To crisp the skin, either leave the door ajar for the last 5 to 10 minutes or pour on a little cold water from time to time during the last 15 minutes (with the door shut).

While the goose is roasting, make the stock with the giblets.

Pour off the fat from the roasting pan and scrape up the cooking juices with the flour. Cook for a minute over high heat. Add the boiling stock; season and add optional marjoram and caraway seeds and simmer for a few minutes. Strain and serve in a sauce boat.

Serves 8.

Roast Turkey with Chestnut Stuffing

At Christmastime we used to put chestnut stuffing in one end and Sausage and Apple (page 143) in the other, using half the quantities given in the recipes. Other stuffings that go well together are Chestnut and Apple (page 142), Sausage and Chestnut (page 141), and Celery, Apple and Walnut (page 143).

Chestnut Stuffing

2½	pounds chestnuts, prepared according to page 135
½	pound salted pork or lean pork belly
2	cups stale bread
1	cup milk
	Turkey giblets, liver, heart, and gizzard
2	tablespoons chopped fresh parsley
	Dash thyme
2	eggs
1	10- to 12-pound turkey
	Coarse salt and freshly ground black pepper
1	stick (4 ounces) butter

Chop chestnuts very fine. If you are using salted pork, chop and simmer for 10 minutes in water to cover; drain. Otherwise chop fresh pork belly.

Meanwhile, soak the bread in the milk. Squeeze dry. In a mixing bowl combine all the ingredients and season.

Season the turkey cavity, put in a little butter, stuff at both ends, and sew up. Truss the turkey. Dot with the butter and cover with foil.

In a preheated slow oven (about 325° F.) roast the turkey for 3½ hours or until cooked. Baste frequently so that it does not dry out. Cook it on its side and turn over halfway through cooking time. Remove the foil to brown the turkey for the last 10 to 15 minutes.

To make a gravy, scrape up the cooking juices with a little dry white wine or Madeira. If you like, serve Cranberry Sauce (page 122) with the turkey. For other ideas see chapter on Sauces and chapter on Garnishes.

Serves 6.

Roast Turkey with Raspberry Sauce

Choose a stuffing from pages 140–144 for the turkey. A stuffing with chestnuts in it goes particularly well.

1	9- to 12-pound turkey, stuffed
1	stick (4 ounces) butter
⅓	cup raspberry jam
3	tablespoons lemon juice
½	cup Madeira or port
⅓	cup stock, chicken, or made from turkey giblets, etc.
	Rind of half a lemon
	Rind of half an orange
1	pint fresh or 2 packages frozen raspberries

Roast the turkey in a preheated 325° F. oven for 2½ hours, dotted with butter and covered with aluminum foil.

Meanwhile, combine the remaining ingredients except the raspberries and simmer until the jam has melted. Pour the sauce over the turkey and roast for another hour or until turkey is cooked, basting frequently. Degrease sauce, strain, and heat through with the raspberries. Serve separately. Serves 6.

Mexican Fruit-Stuffed Turkey

1	10- to 12-pound turkey
1	lemon
	Coarse salt and freshly ground black pepper

Fruit Stuffing

6	strips bacon, diced
1	onion, chopped
2	cloves garlic, chopped
1½	pounds ground pork
3	apples, peeled, cored, and chopped
½	cup tomato purée
8	black olives, pitted and chopped
½	cup raisins
3	bananas, sliced
4	jalapeño chilis, fresh or canned, chopped
2	tablespoons wine vinegar
2	teaspoons sugar
3	cups dry white wine
1	onion, sliced
	Dash thyme
	Dash marjoram
	Bay leaf
4	tablespoons butter

Rub the turkey inside and out with the lemon, salt, and pepper.

Fry the bacon in a heavy skillet and add the onion and garlic. Cook until the onion is soft. Add the pork and cook for about 5 minutes. Add the remaining ingredients for fruit stuffing and simmer about 10 minutes. Stuff into cavity. Sew up and truss turkey.

Arrange the turkey in a roasting pan. Pour on the wine; arrange the onion underneath with the herbs. Dot the turkey with butter, cover with foil, and roast for about 3½ hours in a preheated 325° F. oven. Baste frequently and remove the foil for the last 15 to 20 minutes to brown.

Degrease the cooking juice, scrape up with a little flour if necessary, and serve separately.

Serves 6.

Turkey with Oranges

Plain roast turkey can be very dull, but this way of cooking it gives it an entirely different character. It is good with rice pilaf and a green vegetable.

1	10-pound turkey
	Turkey gizzard, liver, and giblets
	Water to cover
2	carrots, chopped
2	onions, chopped
	Celery leaves
1	orange
4	tablespoons butter
4	stalks celery, chopped
	Coarse salt and freshly ground pepper
	Rosemary
	Oregano
1	stick melted butter
6	sliced bacon strips
1	cup dry white wine or vermouth
	Juice of 2 oranges
1	cup chicken stock
1	clove garlic, chopped
2	tablespoons flour

Remove the wing tips from the turkey and put with the gizzard, liver, and giblets into a pan with water to cover. Add a chopped carrot, a chopped onion, and some celery leaves. Simmer for 20 to 30 minutes, covered.

Dry the turkey with a towel and into the cavity put the orange, unpeeled and diced, 2 tablespoons butter, a chopped onion, carrot, and two celery stalks. Season; add herbs. Brush the bird with some of the melted butter, place the bacon strips over the breast, and cook in a preheated 325° F. oven for 30 minutes.

Baste with remaining butter, wine, orange juice, and stock and season with garlic. Cover loosely with foil and cook until done, basting occasionally.

Remove the turkey to a side dish. Scrape up the cooking juices and bring to boil. In a saucepan melt 2 tablespoons butter and add the flour. Cook together for a minute without browning. Add the cooking juices and bring to boil. Cook until thickened, remove from heat, correct seasoning, and serve in a sauce boat. Sprinkle with parsley.

Serves 6 to 8.

Turkey Mole Poblano

In Mexico this dish is served for a special occasion. It is extremely good for a party since it is inexpensive and is a different way of serving turkey (which can be very dull served stuffed and roasted over and over again). Serve it with guacamole, rice, and beans.

If you cannot get the chilis you need, or you don't have the time to prepare the sauce from scratch, you can buy a mole powder made up of the ground ingredients you need. See the recipe following for quick mole.

1	8- to 9-pound turkey, jointed and cut into pieces
	Water to cover
6	ancho chilis
4	pasillo chilis
6	mulatto chilis
2	slices bread
¾	cup almonds
½	cup shelled peanuts
¾	cup lard
2	onions, chopped
3	tomatoes, peeled and chopped
3	cloves garlic, chopped
½	teaspoon ground cinnamon
½	teaspoon ground cloves
½	teaspoon ground coriander
	Coarse salt and freshly ground black pepper
3	tablespoons sesame seeds

Boil the turkey in water to cover, keeping at a simmer for about an hour. Drain and dry.

Meanwhile, prepare the chilis. Rinse them, remove the skins and seeds, and tear into small pieces. Pour two cups of the turkey broth over them and soak for 30 minutes.

In an electric blender pulverize the bread, almonds, and peanuts with the chilis and their soaking liquid. Heat half the lard in a skillet and brown the turkey. Remove and drain. Add the rest of the lard to the skillet and the blended nuts with the remaining ingredients except the sesame seeds. Add 2 cups of turkey broth and simmer half an hour or until the sauce is very thick.

Arrange the turkey on a serving dish, pour on the sauce, and sprinkle with sesame seed.

Serves 8 to 10.

Short-Cut Mole

This sauce can also be used for pork, chicken, and enchiladas.

1   8- to 9-pound turkey, jointed and cut into pieces
    Water to cover
4   tablespoons lard
2   onions, chopped
6   tomatoes, peeled and chopped
2   cloves garlic, chopped
5   to 6 teaspoons mole powder
    Coarse salt and freshly ground pepper

Cook the turkey as in preceding recipe. In a skillet heat the lard. Add the onion and cook until softened. Add the remaining ingredients except the mole powder and cook for about 20 minutes. Purée in the blender and return to the skillet. Add the powder and 2 cups of turkey broth. Simmer for about half an hour. Spoon over the turkey and serve sprinkled with sesame seeds.

Turkey Wings with Chestnut Purée

This dish can be made with uncooked or cooked turkey wings. If the wings are cooked, you can heat them in the oven with a little stock and butter. Otherwise, the wings are baked in the oven and covered with a little stock. The Chestnut Purée (page 136) is served separately.

Brown the wings gently on each side. Drain. Brown a sliced carrot and an onion with some thyme, bay leaf, and parsley. Return the wings to the casserole and cook in a 325° F. oven, covered. Baste frequently.

Arrange the wings on a serving dish. Add a cupful of stock to the casserole and boil for 15 minutes. Strain and pour over the turkey wings. Serve with chestnut purée. Number of servings depends on how many wings you use.

Meat

Each area of the world seems to have its own particular method of cooking meat with fruits and nuts; this, of course, depends largely on what is available. In the Western countries you find apples, plums, cranberries, chestnuts, and almonds playing a large part. Even in Roman times apples were used in every conceivable way, simmered with meat in stews, used as a garnish, or stuffed into roasts of pork. Pears, too, have long been used for cooking in parts of Europe and go extremely well with ham or bacon. Prunes and plums are used frequently with pork, and cherries have a natural affinity for veal. (They are especially good with the not-so-vealy veal that you get in the United States.) When fruits are not actually cooked with the meat, you find them served as a relish, particularly in Scandinavian and German countries and in England.

In India fruits are used in curries and other spicy dishes to provide a sweet-sour flavor. Nuts such as pistachios, coconuts, and almonds are sprinkled on meat dishes both before and after cooking. Coconut milk forms the "stock" for many stews and curries, as it does in the Caribbean and the Far East, particularly in Thailand and Indonesia. In Latin America, the Caribbean, and the Far East (China, especially) papaya is used not only as a fruit to be cooked with meat but also as a tenderizer. When meat is marinated in papaya pulp or the crushed seeds, it becomes tender. Orange or lemon juice is also used to marinate meats. Chinese cooks stir-fry meat and add nuts or fruits at the end and scrape up the juices into a sauce.

Lamb, with its delicate and slightly sweet flavor, is delicious with apricots or kumquats, as the Persians and Chinese can testify. Of all the meats, pork and ham are perhaps the most versatile as far as cooking with fruit is concerned. They go with just about everything.

Steak in Coconut Cream

This is good way to make steak go further. Rice or noodles are good with it.

1½	pounds steak
3	tablespoons peanut or sesame oil
2	cloves garlic, chopped
6	scallions (plus green part), chopped
2	green or red peppers, chopped
1	teaspoon freshly ground chili pepper
½	teaspoon freshly ground coriander seed
	Dash cumin
	Coarse salt and freshly ground black pepper
½	cup coconut cream (page 130)

Slice the steak in strips about 2 inches long and 1 inch wide. Heat the oil in a skillet and fry the garlic, scallions, and peppers for 2 minutes. Add the meat and spices and brown quickly. Add the coconut cream; season and simmer not more than 5 to 7 minutes so that the meat stays pink inside. It will toughen if you cook it longer.

Serves 4 to 5.

Beef Stew with Cranberries

Serve this stew with rice or boiled potatoes.

2	ounces salt pork, diced
1	tablespoon butter
1	tablespoon olive oil
½	cup shallots, chopped
2	cloves garlic, chopped
2½	pounds stewing beef, cut in 2-inch cubes
	Flour for dredging
1	pound cranberries
2	cups red wine
1	cup beef stock
1	tablespoon brown sugar
	Herb bouquet (thyme, parsley, bay leaf tied in cheesecloth)
	Coarse salt and freshly ground pepper
¼	cup Madeira
1	tablespoon softened butter
	Chopped fresh parsley

In a heavy casserole fry the salt pork in the butter and oil. Add the shallots and the garlic and cook until softened. Roll the beef cubes in flour and brown in the fat. Add the cranberries, wine, stock, sugar, herb bouquet, and seasonings. Cover and simmer for 2 hours or until meat is tender.

Remove meat to a heated serving dish. Strain the sauce through a sieve, squeezing as much juice as you can from the cranberries. In a small saucepan boil up the sauce with the Madeira. Off heat, swirl in the butter enrichment. Pour onto the meat. Sprinkle parsley on top and serve.

Serves 4 to 6.

Beef in Coconut Cream

Variations of this dish show up in Hawaii and Thailand. Rice goes well with it.

4	tablespoons peanut oil
1½	pounds lean beef, cut into strips
1	tablespoon fresh ginger, chopped
2	cloves garlic, chopped
4	scallions, chopped
3	cups coconut cream (see page 130)
2 to 3	dried red chilis, pounded in a mortar
	Coarse salt
1½	pounds fresh spinach, carefully washed, tough stalks removed
1	teaspoon cornstarch
1	tablespoon water

Heat 2 tablespoons of the oil in a large heavy skillet. Brown the beef lightly and add the ginger, garlic, and scallions. Cook for a minute, stirring, then add ¾ cup of coconut cream. Cook for 5 minutes. Add the remaining cream, the chilis and season.

Meanwhile, heat the remaining oil in another frying pan and stir-fry the spinach until it is barely wilted.

Add the cornstarch mixed with 1 tablespoon water to the beef and cook, stirring, until the sauce has thickened.

Put the spinach on a heated plate and pour over the coconut-beef mixture.

Serves 4.

Lamb with Apples and Cherries

Serve this Middle Eastern dish with rice.

2 pounds lamb, cut in 1-inch cubes
2 tablespoons peanut or vegetable oil
  Freshly ground coriander seeds
  Dash thyme
  Dash rosemary
¼ pound yellow lentils
  Coarse salt and freshly ground white pepper
  Water to cover (including cherry juice if canned)
1 pound sour morello cherries, fresh or canned
3 apples
  Squeeze of lemon to taste

Dry the lamb and brown in oil in a heavy saucepan or casserole. Add the herbs, lentils, seasonings, and water to cover. Simmer for about 2 hours, skimming off any scum that rises to the top.

Add the pitted cherries and the apples, peeled, cored, and quartered, and simmer for another 30 minutes. Add lemon juice to taste, correct seasoning, and serve.

Serves 4.

Lamb with Apricots

Lamb and apricots have a special affinity for each other as this Persian recipe shows. The apricots blend their flavor with the meat and bring out the subtle sweetness of the lamb. Serve this over rice.

2 pounds lean lamb, cubed
2 tablespoons butter
1 tablespoon peanut or vegetable oil
1 onion, chopped
¼ teaspoon cinnamon
½ teaspoon freshly ground coriander
  Dash ginger
¼ teaspoon cumin
  Coarse salt and freshly ground pepper
2 tablespoons seedless raisins
¼ pound dried apricots
  Water to cover
  Ground almonds as needed to thicken sauce

Dry the lamb with paper towels. Heat the butter and oil in a heavy fireproof casserole. Gently fry the onion and soften without browning. Add the meat and brown. Add the spices and seasoning. Sauté the raisins and apricots for a few minutes, then add enough water to cover. If you need more room to sauté the fruit, remove the lamb while you do it and return it to the pan.

Cover and stew for about 1½ hours or until the meat is tender. To thicken the sauce, add ground almonds and turn up heat so that the liquid boils down. Correct seasoning and serve with rice.

Serves 4 to 6.

Caribbean Style Kebabs

Papaya is a natural meat tenderizer. If it is available, use it both for the marinade to tenderize and flavor the meat and on the skewers with the pineapple. Otherwise use fresh mangoes or apricots for flavor. On the skewers use more pineapple and banana than is specified. Serve the kebabs over rice with the sauce spooned on top.

This is a good dish to cook on an outdoor grill during the summer.

2   pounds lamb or beef for kebabs
Marinade
   1   tablespoon peanut or vegetable oil
   2   onions, chopped
   2   garlic cloves, chopped
  ½   cup papaya pulp (if available)
   2   tablespoons curry powder
   2   tablespoons vinegar
   2   tablespoons brown sugar
     Coarse salt and freshly ground black pepper
   3   firm ripe bananas or plantains
 12   cubes fresh pineapple
 12   cubes fresh papaya (if available)

Cut the meat into 1½-inch cubes. Set aside.

Heat the oil in a skillet and gently soften the onion with the garlic. Add the remaining ingredients and mix well. Remove from heat and pour over the meat. Toss thoroughly so that each piece is coated; cover and marinate overnight.

Drain and reserve the marinade. Thread the meat and fruit alternately on skewers. Grill under the high heat of a broiler or over charcoal. Combine drippings with marinade, check seasoning, and pour over the kebabs.

Serves 4.

Picadillo

This is a good winter dish. Mashed potatoes or rice goes well with it.

¾   pound ground pork
¾   pound ground veal
2   tablespoons lard or olive oil
1   16-ounce can tomato purée
3   tablespoons raisins
3   tablespoons chopped almonds
1   8-ounce can jalapeño chilis
2   tablespoons finely chopped lemon peel
¼   cup sliced green olives
2   bananas, sliced
4   cloves
1   tablespoon brown sugar
    Dash chili powder
    Dash basil or oregano
    Coarse salt and freshly ground black pepper
2   onions, finely chopped
    Meat or chicken stock if necessary

Brown the meat in the oil. Add the onion and cook over low heat until soft. Add the remaining ingredients and a little stock if more liquid is needed. Cover and simmer gently until the pork is cooked. Correct seasoning and serve. Serves 6.

Casserole Braised Pork with Apricots

3   pounds boneless roast of pork
2   tablespoons butter
1   tablespoon oil
6   shallots, chopped
    Herb bouquet (parsley, bay leaf, thyme tied in cheesecloth)
1   cup stock
    Coarse salt and freshly ground pepper
2   pounds fresh apricots
1   cup white wine
    Chopped fresh parsley

In a fireproof casserole brown the pork in the butter and oil on top of the stove. Remove and cook the shallots without browning for 5 minutes. Return the pork with the herb bouquet and stock and cook in a preheated 325° F. oven for 1 hour.

Add the apricots with a little of the wine if necessary. Cover and cook another hour, or until done, basting occasionally.

Transfer the pork to a heated plate. Arrange the apricots around it. Degrease the sauce and boil it down with the rest of the wine. Correct seasoning, scatter on some chopped fresh parsley, and serve separately.

Serves 6.

Note: Dried apricots, soaked overnight in water or white wine, can be used in place of fresh ones. Cook them for 1½ to 2 hours with the pork.

Pork Chops with Bananas

4 loin chops
1 tablespoon olive oil
2 tablespoons butter
8 bananas
   Lemon juice
   Freshly grated nutmeg
   Coarse salt and freshly ground pepper
4 tablespoons unsalted roasted almonds, chopped
   Chopped fresh parsley to garnish

Trim the chops. Heat 1 tablespoon butter and the oil in a heavy pan that has a lid. Brown the chops on either side, cover, turn down the heat, and cook for about 20 minutes or until done.

Meanwhile, peel and slice bananas. Mash in a bowl with lemon juice. Heat the remaining butter in another pan and cook the bananas over low heat. Season and put on a heated dish. Squeeze some more lemon on top and grate a little nutmeg over them. Place the chops on top, season, and sprinkle almonds and chopped parsley over the top.

Serves 4.

Pork Chops with Brazil Nuts

Baked sweet potatoes or rice goes very well with these chops. They improve the longer they are marinated, and I suggest you try to keep them in the marinade, turning occasionally, for a couple of days.

 4   thick-cut pork chops
Marinade

   About 10 Brazil nuts, grated or pulverized in the blender
 1   tablespoon ground coriander
 1   clove garlic, mashed
 1   tablespoon chili powder
 ¼   cup soy sauce
   Juice of half a lemon
 2   tablespoons brown sugar
 2   tablespoons peanut or olive oil
   Coarse salt and freshly ground black pepper

Trim, wash, and dry the pork chops. In a mixing bowl combine the remaining ingredients. Pour over chops and marinade for 2 days or at least 8 hours, turning them occasionally. Heat the oven to 375° F. and bake the chops in their sauce for about 40 minutes or until they are done. Correct seasoning and serve.

Serves 4.

Spareribs with Pineapple

Serve this Chinese dish with rice. The ribs will taste twice as good if you marinate them overnight in the soy sauce.

Get the butcher to cut up the ribs for you if you don't possess a cleaver.

 2   pounds pork spareribs, cut in 2-inch pieces
 ¼   cup soy sauce
 2   cloves garlic, chopped
 1   tablespoon chopped fresh ginger
 1   cup pineapple juice
 ¼   cup brown sugar
 ¼   cup vinegar
 2   tablespoons peanut or sesame oil
 1   green pepper, thinly sliced
 1   cup pineapple chunks
   Coarse salt and freshly ground pepper
 1   tablespoon cornstarch
 1   tablespoon water

Put the ribs in a bowl with the soy sauce, garlic, and ginger and turn well in the mixture. Leave overnight if possible or 6 hours at room temperature.

Mix the pineapple juice with the sugar and vinegar.

Heat the oil in a heavy skillet. Dry the ribs with paper towels and brown in the oil. Add the pepper and cook for a minute. Add the pineapple juice mixture and simmer, covered, for about 45 minutes. Add the pineapple chunks, salt and pepper, and heat through.

Meanwhile, blend the cornstarch with water. Add to the pan and when the sauce has thickened remove from heat and serve.

Serves 4.

Roast Pork with Lemons and Oranges

1   pork loin
6   anchovies
1   stick butter at room temperature
    Dash thyme
    Dash mace
    Coarse salt and freshly ground black pepper
2   onions, sliced
2   oranges, sliced
2   lemons, sliced
1   cup white wine
½   cup meat stock
    Freshly chopped parsley

Make little slits in the pork and insert pieces of anchovies. Mix the butter thoroughly with the herbs and seasonings and spread over the roast, putting a little in the bottom of the roasting pan, too. Arrange the onions and orange and lemon slices around the roast and cook in a preheated 400° F. oven for half an hour. Add the wine and the stock. Turn the oven down to 350° F. and continue cooking until the pork is done (about 2 hours). Pour the fat off the cooking juices and serve the gravy separately with parsley scattered over the top.

Orange Pork Risotto

Served with a green vegetable or salad, this makes a warming and economical meal for a cold day. You can use up leftover pork and other chopped leftovers by adding them to the rice. The combination of orange and tomato gives it a distinctive flavor, and when cooked, the mixture turns a marvelous deep orange-red that makes an attractive contrast with the yellow of the bananas and the green of the parsley.

> 1 pound diced pork (or 2 cups leftover pork)
> 2 tablespoons peanut or vegetable oil
> 4 large, juicy tomatoes, chopped
> 1 cup orange juice
> ½ cup dry sherry
> Dash basil
> Dash curry powder
> 1 cup rice
> Hot water or stock as necessary
> 4 to 6 bananas, sliced
> 1 can or 1 cup cooked red beans (optional)
> Coarse salt and freshly ground pepper
> Chopped fresh parsley

If the pork is raw, fry it in the oil and set aside. In a deep heavy pan put the chopped tomatoes, orange juice, sherry, and spices. Cover and bring to boil. Simmer until the tomatoes are cooked. Mash them with a fork so that there are no big lumps. Add the rice, seasonings, and about a cup of water or stock. Stir. Add the pork and cover and simmer until the rice is cooked, adding more water as needed.

Meanwhile, fry the bananas in the skillet in which you cooked the pork, with more oil if you need it.

When the rice mixture is cooked add the beans if you like, to heat through. Arrange the bananas over the top, scatter on some chopped fresh parsley, season, and serve.

Serves 4 to 6.

Note: Chopped fresh peanuts are delicious scattered on top of the rice mixture.

Stir-Fried Pork with Peanuts

Rice is good with this Chinese dish.

> 2 pounds lean pork
> 2 tablespoons cornstarch
> 3 tablespoons soy sauce
> ¼ cup dry sherry
> 1 cup unsalted peanuts
> 4 to 6 tablespoons peanut or sesame oil
> 1 garlic clove, chopped
> 3 scallions, minced (including green part)
> ½ pound mushrooms, chopped
> 2 to 3 tablespoons oyster sauce
> 1 cup meat stock

Dice the pork. Toss in a mixture of the cornstarch mixed to a paste with the soy sauce and the sherry.

Heat the oil in a large, heavy skillet. Salt the peanuts and brown them in the oil. Drain on paper towels. Add the remaining oil. Sauté the garlic and scallions for a minute. Add the pork and stir-fry for about 5 minutes. Add the mushrooms, cook for a minute, then add the oyster sauce and stock. Bring to boil, turn down heat, and cover. Cook until the pork is done (about 10 to 15 minutes).

Stir in peanuts to reheat, and serve.

Serves 4.

Baked Ham and Banana Rolls

This Caribbean dish is an excellent way to use up ham. It makes a good little supper dish on its own with a green salad to follow.

8	thin slices ham
	Dark mustard
8	bananas

Sauce

1	tablespoon butter
1	tablespoon flour
1½	cups milk
2 to 3	tablespoons freshly grated cheddar cheese
	Coarse salt and freshly ground pepper
	Freshly grated nutmeg

Spread the ham slices with mustard and wrap around a peeled banana.

Melt the butter in a saucepan, add the flour, and cook together without browning for a couple of minutes. Meanwhile, bring the milk to a boil and add all at once to the butter-flour mixture, stirring vigorously. Add the cheese and stir until the sauce has thickened and the cheese has melted. Season and pour on the ham rolls. Sprinkle with nutmeg and bake in a preheated 350° F. oven for about 10 to 15 minutes.

Serves 4.

Veal Stew with Peanuts

This is a good way to cook the darker cuts of veal. Sautéed escarole, spinach, zucchini, or broccoli is good with it.

Grind the peanuts in a blender or with a pestle and mortar.

```
2   pounds stewing veal, cut in 2-inch cubes
2   tablespoons butter
2   tablespoons oil
2   cloves garlic, finely chopped
1   onion, finely chopped
4   tomatoes, peeled and chopped
    Dash basil (fresh if available)
2   cups chicken stock
1½  cups ground fresh unsalted peanuts
    Coarse salt and freshly ground white pepper
    Chopped fresh parsley for decoration
```

Dry the veal with paper towels. In a casserole heat the butter and the oil. Brown the veal without burning. Add the garlic and the onion, turn down the heat, and cook until the onion is clear. Add the remaining ingredients (except the parsley) and cook over low heat, covered, for about 25 minutes, adding more stock or water if necessary. Correct seasoning, sprinkle with parsley, and serve.

Enough for 6.

Veal Escalopes Stuffed with Pine Nuts

A potato casserole would be good with this Italian dish.

```
8    veal escalopes
8    thin slices prosciutto
¼    cup pine nuts
1    tablespoon olive oil
2    tablespoons raisins
2    tablespoons freshly grated Parmesan cheese
2    tablespoons chopped fresh parsley
     Coarse salt and freshly ground pepper
2    tablespoons butter
½ to ¾  cup dry white wine
```

Pound the veal with the flat side of a knife. Lay a slice of prosciutto on each slice of veal.

Sauté the pine nuts in the oil.

Spread the pine nuts mixed with the raisins, cheese, parsley, and seasonings on the meat. Roll up, cut in half, and secure each roll with a toothpick.

Heat the butter in a large skillet. Brown the rolls lightly, add the wine, cover and simmer for 15 to 20 minutes, or until done.

Serves 4.

Russian Veal with Sour Cherries

This is especially good if you can make it with fresh sour cherries. Serve it with boiled or mashed potatoes.

You need an ovenproof casserole with a tight-fitting lid to make this successfully.

    1   3- to 4-pound veal rump or leg
        Coarse salt and freshly ground pepper
    ½   pound sour cherries
    2   tablespoons butter, melted
    1   tablespoon cardamom seeds
    ½   teaspoon ground cinnamon
        Flour
    ½   cup white wine
    ½   cup cherry juice
    1   cup chicken or meat stock

Dry the meat and rub with salt and pepper. With the point of a knife make incisions all over the joint. Put a stoned cherry in each hole. Place the veal in a roasting dish and sprinkle with melted butter, cardamom, and cinnamon. Roast in a preheated 450° F. oven to brown. When browned, sprinkle with flour and turn oven down to 350° F. Cook for 20 minutes.

Add the wine, cherry juice, and stock. Baste frequently and roast for about 1¾ hours or until done.

Serves 6.

Veal Chops with Pecan Sauce

This is very good served on a bed of puréed or chopped spinach.

        6   thick-cut veal chops
        1   clove garlic, finely chopped
        3   tablespoons butter
            Dash thyme
        1   onion, finely chopped
    ½ to 1   cup chicken stock
        1   cup finely chopped pecans
        ½   cup heavy cream
            Coarse salt and freshly ground white pepper
            Chopped fresh parsley for decoration

Brown the chops with the garlic in the butter without burning. Remove to a warm platter. Add the thyme and onion and cook over low heat until the onion is soft. Return the chops to the casserole with about half a cup of the stock, adding more if necessary to keep the chops moist. Cook until the chops are almost done. Add the pecans, remaining seasonings, and more stock if it is dry. Simmer gently for about 5 minutes. Add the cream and heat through. Decorate with parsley and serve.

Serves 6.

Veal with Pecans and Sour Cream

This is a delicious veal stew, a little like a goulash but without the paprika. Serve potatoes and a green vegetable with it.

2   pounds stewing veal, cut up and tossed in seasoned flour
2   tablespoons butter
2   tablespoons olive oil
1   onion, chopped
2   cloves garlic, mashed
    Dash thyme
    Dash oregano
1   cup white wine
1   cup chicken broth
1   cup shelled pecans
2   tablespoons butter
    Coarse salt and freshly ground black pepper
½   cup sour cream
¼   cup chopped fresh parsley or dill
    Lemon juice to taste

Dry the veal on paper towels. Heat the butter and oil in the casserole and add the veal. Brown and set aside. Add the onion, garlic, and spices and cook for about 5 minutes. Return the veal to the casserole and add the wine and broth. Cook for about 1½ hours. Sauté the pecans in the butter. Add the liquid from the veal stew and blend in the blender at high speed until the nuts are pulverized into the juice. Return to the casserole, adding salt and pepper, and bring to simmer. Cook for about 15 minutes, add the cream, parsley, and lemon, correct seasoning, and serve.

Serves 4 to 6.

Birnen, Bohnen, und Speck

This is a traditional German dish, and it is excellent as a light supper.

6   pears
½   cup water
1   pound string beans, trimmed
    Lemon peel
    Thyme
6   strips bacon
4   tablespoons sugar
2   tablespoons vinegar
    Lemon juice
    Coarse salt and freshly ground pepper

Peel, core, and slice the pears. Cook them in the water for 10 minutes, then add the beans. Cook until they are almost done.

Meanwhile, fry the bacon. Remove from the pan and drain on paper towels. Add the vegetables, toss in the fat, and add the remaining ingredients. Cover and simmer until the beans are cooked. Crumble the bacon over the vegetables and serve.

Serves 4.

Liver with Oranges

Serve this over rice, which you might sprinkle with a little freshly grated Parmesan if you like.

1   orange
2   tablespoons butter
1   tablespoon olive oil
1   onion, chopped
2   cloves garlic, chopped
    Dash thyme
    About 3 tablespoons flour
1   teaspoon dry mustard
    Dash cayenne pepper
    Coarse salt
8   slices calf's liver
½   cup red wine
½   cup meat stock
    Chopped parsley to garnish

Peel the orange very thin, cut the peel into *julienne* (thin strips), and drop into boiling water for 5 minutes. Drain and set aside. Reserve the orange.

Melt 1 tablespoon butter and the oil in a frying pan. Soften the onion with the garlic over low heat. Remove to a small plate.

Combine the flour with the mustard and seasonings. Roll the liver in this mixture. Heat the remaining butter in the frying pan and fry the liver lightly on each side so that it is pink in the middle. Remove to a heated dish. Return the onions to the pan with the red wine and stock. Turn heat up high and reduce the liquid. Meanwhile, slice the orange and add. Cook for about 1 minute.

Arrange the liver over the rice and spoon the sauce on top with the sliced orange. Garnish with parsley.

Serves 4.

Liver with Apples

1½   pounds calf's liver, sliced
1½   pounds tart cooking apples
4   ounces butter (1 stick)
    Coarse salt and freshly ground black pepper
    Dash powdered thyme
    Flour
1   tablespoon apple brandy or other brandy
    Chopped fresh parsley to garnish

Trim the filament from the liver. Set aside. Peel, core, and slice the apples. Heat half the butter in a frying pan and gently cook the apples, just enough to soften them. Meanwhile, season the liver and dredge with flour. Heat the remaining butter in another skillet and fry the liver lightly, about 3 minutes on each side so that it is pink in the middle.

Put the liver on a heated dish. Add the brandy to the apples and light with a match. Arrange the apples around the liver, decorate with parsley, and serve.

Enough for 4.

Rabbit with Prunes

1   rabbit, cut up into serving pieces
2   cups good red wine
3   carrots, sliced
1   onion, sliced
1   bay leaf
    Herb bouquet (thyme, parsley, bay leaf tied in cheesecloth)
    Coarse salt and freshly ground pepper
2   tablespoons butter
2   tablespoons olive oil
¾   pound prunes, soaked overnight in water to cover
2   tablespoons red currant jelly

Marinate the rabbit overnight in a glass, china, or enamel dish in the wine with the carrots, onion, herbs, and seasoning. Drain and reserve marinade. Heat the butter and oil and brown the rabbit pieces that you have patted dry with a towel. Add the marinade and prune water to cover. Add the prunes, bring to boil, and simmer for an hour, skimming off any foam that may rise to the top. Just before serving, correct seasoning and stir in the red currant jelly.

Enough for 4.

Tongue with Peanuts

To make this dish correctly, you must make your own peanut butter. It is not difficult, but it requires a blender. Once you have made this butter, you will never regret it because it makes the store-bought kind seem like a completely different food. I suggest you make twice the amount suggested here and keep it for other dishes or to eat by itself.

    About 10 to 12 slices cooked tongue
¼   pound raw shelled peanuts, skins on
¼ to ½   cup peanut oil
    Coarse salt and freshly ground black pepper
2   tablespoons butter
1   medium-sized onion
1   clove garlic
    Dash cinnamon
¼   cup chopped fresh parsley

Trim the tongue. In a blender put the peanuts, add the oil gradually, blending and adding more as you need it, season, and set aside. Heat the butter in the skillet. Sauté the tongue slices lightly and remove to a heated dish. Soften the onion and garlic. Add the cinnamon and the peanut butter. Return the tongue to the pan. Correct seasoning and scatter parsley over the top.

Serves 4.

Tongue with Almond Sauce

1   2-pound calf's tongue
1   onion, coarsely chopped
2   carrots, coarsely chopped
   Bay leaf
   Celery stalk and leaves, chopped
   Water to cover

Almond Sauce

4   tomatoes, chopped
¾   cup ground almonds
4   hard-boiled eggs
3   tablespoons finely chopped parsley
   Dry red or white wine, stock, or water
1   tablespoon finely chopped fresh basil (or ½ tablespoon dried)
   Coarse salt and freshly ground black pepper
½   cup olive oil
1   tablespoon white wine vinegar

Cook the tongue with the vegetables and water to cover until tender. Drain, skin, and slice.

Put the tomatoes into a heavy saucepan with the almonds, hard-boiled egg yolks (mashed), herbs, and seasonings. Cover and simmer gently until thick, adding a little liquid if it seems too dry. Remove from heat and add the oil, vinegar, and the chopped whites. If it needs more liquid, add extra oil or extra liquid as you please. Correct seasoning and pour over the tongue. Decorate with extra parsley and serve.

Tongue Veronique

Serve this with mashed potatoes. Make the sauce while the tongue is cooking and pour it over the sliced tongue while it is still hot.

1   4-pound beef tongue (or 6 lamb's tongues), cooked (see above)

Sauce

1   tablespoon butter
2   shallots, chopped
1   carrot, chopped
2   tablespoons flour
2   ounces chopped mushrooms
1   teaspoon tomato purée
1   pint meat stock
     Herb bouquet (thyme, parsley, bay leaf tied in cheesecloth)
1   glass Madeira or sherry
     Coarse salt and freshly ground pepper
4   ounces seedless grapes
2   ounces almonds, slivered

Melt the butter and brown the shallots with the carrot. Add the flour and brown. Add the mushrooms with the tomato purée, stock, and herbs and simmer for 30 to 40 minutes. Strain and return to the pan with the Madeira. Simmer until thick, then add the grapes and almonds, salt and pepper. Correct seasoning.

Slice the tongue and pour the sauce over.

Serves 4 to 6.

Sauces and Butters

Plain cooked meat, poultry, fish, or vegetables can be greatly enhanced by a fruit or nut sauce. Cold food is also good with a fairly strong sauce to accompany it. This chapter contains sauces from all parts of the world, from the American chestnut, cranberry, and grape sauces to the Chinese duk sauce and the Russian tkemali sauce (both made from plums). Closer to home, the Germans have their apple sauces and the English their famous Cumberland sauce, while the West Indies makes sauces from peanuts and coconut milk. In Latin America sauces are often thickened with ground nuts or pumpkin seed. I have found this in many cases to be much better than cornstarch or flour. Ground almonds are very good with light mild sauces, whereas ground pumpkin seeds go well in strong spicy sauces. You can pulverize nuts in a blender and keep them in a sealed jar in the refrigerator so that you can use them as you need them. Sauces thickened this way are particularly good with vegetables.

You will also find some pastes from the Middle East that can be either eaten as an hors d'oeuvre with flat Arabic bread or thinned down into a delicious sauce for fish or chicken.

Marinades soften the tough fibers of meat or chicken and give it a delicious flavor. In both the Caribbean and Latin America papaya and fruit juices are used to tenderize meat. Papaya, in fact, is a natural meat tenderizer and is used in the commercial preparation. I would not buy the commercial stuff, being a bug about chemicals in my food, but I would recommend the natural method with papaya pulp or seeds.

Savory butters can be used both in sauces and to flavor stews and can be spread on bread for canapés to give flavor. Sweet butters can also be used on bread, either by themselves or combined with other foods, such as ham with apple butter, pork with apricot butter, cream cheese with prune butter, and so on. These butters can also be used as fillings for cakes.

Sweet fruit sauces can be used for pancakes, fritters, and steamed or baked puddings. They can be served hot or cold.

120

Applesauce

Serve applesauce with sausages, chops, goose, roast pork, mutton, and other roast meats.

Chopped almonds, an onion softened in butter, grated orange or lemon peel, brown sugar, spices such as cinnamon, mace, nutmeg, cardamom, and white wine can also be added to the sauce.

Do not salt applesauce.

1   pound cooking apples
¼   cup sugar
2   tablespoons butter (optional)

Peel, core, and quarter the apples. Put them in a heavy saucepan with the sugar. Cover and cook over low heat until soft. Add the butter and cook until melted. Serve hot or cold.

Chestnut Sauce

For chicken and turkey (especially good with cold turkey).

2   dozen chestnuts
2   cups meat or chicken stock
    Thyme
    Salt and freshly ground black pepper
    Sherry

Boil 2 dozen chestnuts in their skins until they are tender. While they are hot, peel the shells and inner skin. Rub them through a large-grained sieve and return them to the saucepan with the stock. Simmer for 20 minutes, adding a little thyme, and salt and pepper to taste. Remove from heat and stir in a small glass of sherry. Serve hot.

Chestnut and Red Wine Sauce

For roast beef.

2   dozen chestnuts
2   tablespoons butter
1   teaspoon sugar
1   cup red wine
1   cup meat stock

Prepare the chestnuts as for the Chestnut Sauce and return them to the pan with the butter, sugar, red wine, and stock. Season and simmer until the chestnuts are soft and red. Serve hot.

Cranberry Sauce

Cranberry Sauce is traditionally served with roast turkey. You can also serve it with game and roast chicken. Interesting variations can be made by adding white wine in place of water, the juice and grated peel of an orange or lemon, spices, or peeled, cored, and quartered apples to the compote.

1 pound cranberries
1 cup sugar
2 cups water

Put the cranberries, sugar, and water into a pan and cook until tender. Sieve and serve hot or cold.

You can also serve the sauce without sieving it, as a compote.

Cranberry-Walnut Sauce

4 cups fresh cranberries
1 cup fresh orange juice
2 cups sugar
½ teaspoon cinnamon
½ teaspoon ground ginger
½ cup chopped walnuts

Simmer the fresh cranberries in the orange juice for 5 minutes. Add sugar, cinnamon, and ground ginger. Bring to boil and cool. Strain and mix in the chopped walnuts. Serve with cold turkey, chicken, or game.

Duk Sauce (Chinese Plum Sauce)

This sauce can be kept in a tightly sealed jar. Serve in small condiment dishes as an accompaniment to Chinese or Indian meals.

½ cup chutney
1 cup plum jam
1 tablespoon brown sugar
1 tablespoon wine vinegar

Combine all the ingredients in a saucepan and heat through. Add water if the mixture is too thick. Serve cold.

Grape Sauce

For ham, chicken, or fish.

  2   tablespoons butter
  2   tablespoons flour
  1   cup hot chicken or fish stock
  2   egg yolks
 ½   cup seedless grapes
     Coarse salt and freshly ground white pepper
     Lemon juice to taste

Heat the butter in a saucepan and add the flour. Cook together without browning for a couple of minutes. Add the stock and bring to boil, stirring constantly. Off heat, beat in egg yolks and add the grapes. Heat through over *very* low heat. Correct seasoning.

Sauce Maltaise

This is a hollandaise sauce flavored with orange juice. It is very good with asparagus or broccoli.

 ¼   pound butter
  1   orange
  3   egg yolks
  1   lemon
     Coarse salt and white pepper
  1   tablespoon cold water

Melt the butter, reserving two pieces (about 1 tablespoon each) on the side. Grate the peel of the orange and in a bowl whisk it with the egg yolks until they are thick and creamy. Add a tablespoon each lemon and orange juice. Season and set over boiling water with a little butter. Or you can put the mixture into a heavy saucepan over a low flame, but be very careful not to get the sauce too hot or it will curdle.

Keep whisking and adding butter until the sauce becomes a thick cream, taking it off the heat every now and again if you feel it is getting too hot. At the end add the unmelted butter. Thin out the sauce with more orange or lemon juice if it is too thick. Serve hot in a sauceboat. (Don't pour it directly on the vegetables; their liquid may make it runny.)

Cumberland Sauce

Cold meat such as ham, tongue, beef, venison, and mutton are good with this sauce. It can be kept for several weeks in the refrigerator in a tightly sealed jar.

2 shallots, chopped
2 large oranges
4 tablespoons red currant jelly
1 teaspoon French mustard
Coarse salt
Cayenne pepper
Ground ginger (optional)
½ cup port

Simmer the shallots in water for about 5 minutes. Drain and squeeze dry with paper towels.

With a paring knife peel the oranges very thin. Chop the peel finely and simmer in water for 5 minutes.

Combine all the ingredients in a bowl, except the port, and heat through over boiling water until a smooth paste. Add the port and cook for another 5 minutes. Cool and chill.

Peanut Sauce

For chicken, tongue, ham and lamb, or pork kidneys.

1 cup peanuts
Peanut oil
¼ cup minced onion
1 ounce butter
1 cup chicken stock
Coarse salt and freshly ground pepper
Brown sugar

Grind the peanuts in the blender with a little oil so that the mixture is like peanut butter. Soften the onion in the butter and add the peanuts and the stock. Simmer gently. Add brown sugar and salt and pepper to taste.

Sour Plum Sauce (Tkemali)

This Russian sauce tastes rather like an exotic cranberry sauce. It is very good with chicken, goose, turkey, duck, and pork. Sour cooking plums are the best to use.

Fresh coriander is obtainable in Latin American and Chinese shops. If you can't get it, use fresh parsley and dried, crushed coriander seed.

½ pound tart cooking plums
¼ cup water
4 tablespoons chopped fresh coriander
1 clove garlic, crushed
1 teaspoon cayenne pepper
 Coarse salt

Put all the ingredients in a saucepan and simmer gently for about 15 minutes. Take the stones out of the sauce (either sieve the sauce or pick them out) and serve either hot or cold. Makes about 1 cup.

Russian Sour Prune Sauce

Serve this with skewered lamb or fried chicken.

1 pound dried prunes
 Water to cover
1 clove garlic
2 tablespoons chopped fresh coriander
 Coarse salt and freshly ground pepper
 Lemon juice to taste

If possible, soak the prunes overnight in the water. Bring to boil and simmer until cooked. Pit the prunes and combine in the blender with the remaining ingredients. Add the prune liquid. Purée and return to the saucepan. Bring to boil, correct seasoning, and add lemon juice. Cool to room temperature before serving.

Prune Sauce II

For pork, venison, or mutton.

Boil the prunes as above. Pit and combine in blender with 1 tablespoon sugar and 1 tablespoon brandy. If a thinner sauce is preferred, sieve the prunes and then combine with the brandy and sugar.

125

Almond Parsley Sauce

This Mexican sauce is good with fish and chicken.

1	cup chopped fresh parsley
¼	cup blanched almonds
1	clove garlic (optional)
3	tablespoons wine vinegar
½	cup olive oil
	Coarse salt and freshly ground white pepper
	Squeeze of lemon to taste (optional)

Mix all the ingredients together and cook slowly over low heat until the parsley is tender. Put in blender and purée. Correct seasoning.

Apple-Horseradish Sauce

This German sauce goes with veal or pork, ham, fish, and beef (especially cold beef).

1	pound cooking apples
1 to 2	tablespoons sugar
1 to 2	tablespoons grated horseradish
	Few drops of lemon juice or vinegar to taste

Cook the apples in their skins until they are soft. Put through a sieve. Return the purée to the saucepan with the remaining ingredients, heat through, and cool. Serve cold.

Note: An interesting variation of this sauce can be made by adding the chopped yolks and whites of 2 hard-boiled eggs and a tablespoon of capers. Moisten with a little mayonnaise.

Tahini Paste

You can buy sesame paste in most specialty stores. It's even available in some supermarkets.

You can make it thin or thick according to how much oil and lemon you put in it. It can be used as an hors d'oeuvre with Arabic bread, raw as a dip for vegetables, or as a sauce for fish.

    1   **cup sesame paste**
3 to 4   **cloves garlic, crushed**
         Juice of a lemon according to taste
         Olive oil
         Chopped parsley to garnish

Mix the sesame paste with the garlic and lemon juice. Add olive oil and mix to desired consistency. Garnish with parsley and serve.

Tahini with Almonds

Serve this with Arabic bread, cold chicken, and fish.

       Tahini Paste, see above
⅓   **cup ground almonds**
½   **teaspoon sugar**
       Whole almonds to decorate
       Chopped parsley to garnish

Use a blender or electric mixer and combine all the ingredients except the whole almonds and parsley. Blend and place in a bowl. Garnish with the almonds and parsley.

Tahini with Walnuts

This is good with fish, beans, or cauliflower, and as a sauce for cold, cooked vegetables.

To one cup tahini paste, add ¼ pound walnuts. Mix in the blender (don't overblend) with a little warm water.

Almond Paste

For cold fish or chicken.

   2   **cups blanched almonds**
   1   **clove garlic, finely chopped**
   1   **teaspoon sugar**
      Coarse salt and freshly ground pepper
      Juice of 1½ to 2 lemons
   3   **tablespoons peanut, sesame, or almond oil**
   3   **tablespoons parsley or coriander**

Either grind the almonds in the blender or pulverize them with a mortar and pestle, setting aside a few to garnish. Add the garlic, sugar, and seasonings. Gradually add the lemon juice, beating with a fork. When the mixture is a smooth paste, add oil, correct seasoning and put in a bowl. Garnish with almonds and chopped fresh parsley.

Almond Mustard Sauce

For fried, poached or baked fish.

1 cup almonds
1 tablespoon dark mustard
1 tablespoon white wine vinegar
   Coarse salt and freshly ground black pepper

Pulverize almonds in a blender or with a mortar and pestle. Add about 1 tablespoon each dark mustard and white wine vinegar, or more to taste. Season with coarse salt and freshly ground pepper. Add cold water as necessary to thin out the sauce.

Almond Butter

For hors d'oeuvres and canapés and to flavor sauces, creams, and soups. Also good with fish or chicken.

Pound to a paste 1 cup blanched almonds with a few drops of cold water in a mortar. Continue to pound and add ½ pound soft butter. Sieve and refrigerate.

Hazelnut Butter

Same as almond butter, using hazelnuts instead.

Pistachio Butter

Same as almond butter. Peel the pistachio nuts but don't blanch. Use with fish or chicken and on liver pâté canapés.

Almond Butter Sauce

For poached or broiled fish, broccoli, green beans, and peas. Cook 1 cup shredded blanched almonds in 4 ounces butter until golden. Stir constantly.

Orange Butter

Use with baked or grilled fish. Red snapper or pompano is particularly good with it.

½ stick butter
Grated rind of 1 orange
2 teaspoons orange juice
Coarse salt
Hungarian paprika

Work half a stick of butter (2 ounces) at room temperature to a cream. Add the grated rind of an orange, orange juice, coarse salt, and some good Hungarian paprika. Mix well and form into a square or ball. Refrigerate so that it will harden.

Orange and Lemon Marinade

For pork or chicken.

Juice 2 oranges
Juice 1 lemon
1 clove garlic, crushed
Thyme, bay leaf, parsley
Peppercorns

Combine the ingredients, adding more juice if necessary. Pour over the meat and make sure it is covered with the marinade. Leave overnight.

Papaya Seed Marinade

Papaya is a natural meat tenderizer, as people who come from areas in which it is grown know well. Both the pulp and the seeds can be used.

The tough fibers of the meat are broken down, and it becomes both tender and more digestible.

This marinade is particularly good for tough cuts of beef, especially steak.

4 tablespoons papaya seeds
1 teaspoon mustard
1 clove garlic, chopped
4 tablespoons red wine
2 tablespoons oil
Freshly ground pepper

Grind the papaya seeds in a blender or with a pestle and mortar. Combine with the remaining ingredients and coat the meat. Leave overnight or at least 6 hours. When ready to cook the meat, scrape off with paper towels. Enough for 1½ pounds meat.

Yogurt-Papaya Marinade

This is particularly good for lamb as well as beef and pork.

½ cup papaya pulp
4 tablespoons yogurt
1 clove garlic, chopped
1 tablespoon soy sauce
1 teaspoon dark mustard
Freshly ground pepper

Combine the ingredients and spread on the meat. Leave overnight or at least 6 hours. Enough for 2 pounds meat.

Coconut Cream

Although unsweetened coconut cream can be bought canned, it is fiendishly expensive and not nearly so good as homemade, which costs about a quarter as much. It is not complicated to make, particularly if you have a blender.

Apart from its use in recipes throughout this book, coconut cream is also extremely good in curries instead of stock and indeed in many dishes in which coconut cream instead of meat or chicken stock would seem appropriate.

Pierce 2 of the 3 eyes of a fresh coconut. Pour the milk into a cup.

Preheat the oven to 400° F. and bake the coconut for 15 minutes. Remove it, put it on a hard surface, and split it with a hammer. The meat should come off easily.

You can now either grate the coconut, grind it in a mincing machine or coffee mill, or put it with the milk in a blender and blend it coarsely.

Pour the coconut into a cheesecloth with the milk and let the liquid drip through, squeezing the cloth several times. The cream will keep for a few days in a tightly covered container.

The cream from 1 coconut will probably amount to less than a cup. You can add water or milk to the coconut in the cheesecloth to make up the required amount. More than 2 cups calls for 2 coconuts.

Desiccated coconut can be used with milk or water, but the resultant cream will be much thinner. Soak in the *hot* liquid for an hour and then squeeze through a cheesecloth as for fresh coconut cream.

Mayonnaise with Nuts

Good with tomatoes (chop in a little fresh basil if you have it), cold chicken, fish, or shrimp.

    1   cup nuts (hazelnuts, walnuts, or Brazil nuts)
    1½   cups homemade mayonnaise
         Lemon juice
         Dash brown sugar
         Coarse salt
         Freshly ground black pepper

Roast 1 cup hazelnuts, walnuts, or Brazil nuts (or a mixture of these) in the oven for 15 minutes at 300° F. Put them through a coffee grinder, blender, or food mill. Make 1½ cups homemade mayonnaise and add the nuts. Season with lemon juice to taste, a dash of brown sugar, coarse salt, and freshly ground pepper.

Apple Butter

Slow cooking will develop the flavors of fruit butters and enable the oil of the spices to blend with the juices of the fruits. The butter is done when a rim of liquid no longer separates from the butter when you put some on a plate.

This butter is excellent with cream cheese on black bread.

1½ quarts apple cider (unpasteurized if possible)
4 pounds apples, peeled and chopped
1 cup brown sugar
1 teaspoon cinnamon
¼ teaspoon allspice
¼ teaspoon nutmeg
About 6 cardamom seeds, crushed and ground
¼ teaspoon powdered cloves
Dash salt

Boil the cider for 30 minutes. Add the apples and cook slowly until soft but not pulpy. Stir continuously. When cooked, put the mixture through a sieve or purée in a blender. Add the remaining ingredients and cook for a further 45 minutes, stirring continuously. Put into jars and seal. Makes about 2 pints.

Apricot Pineapple Butter

1 pound dried apricots soaked overnight in water to cover
1 can crushed pineapple and its juice
2 oranges
1 lemon
1 cup sugar or honey

Simmer the apricots in the water until soft. Put them in the blender with the pineapple and the juice (and the cooking liquid). Return purée to saucepan and add the juice of the oranges and lemon. Stir in the sugar and cook until thick. Pour into jars and store in a cool place.

Prune Butter

1 pound prunes, soaked overnight in water to cover
Finely chopped peel of an orange
1 cup sugar or honey
¼ teaspoon powdered allspice
¼ teaspoon ginger
¼ teaspoon grated nutmeg
¼ teaspoon powdered cinnamon

Bring prunes to boil in the water and cook until soft. Simmer orange peel in water 10 minutes. Pit and put in blender with their juice. Purée and return to saucepan with the remaining ingredients. Cook until smooth; put into jars and seal. Store in a cool place.

Almond Sauce

1 ounce almonds
  Orange flower water
¼ pint cream
2 egg yolks
  Sugar to taste

Pulverize the almonds with a little orange flower water in a mortar. Put into a saucepan with the cream. Over low heat add the beaten eggs and whisk until thick. Add sugar to taste.

Apricot Sauce

12 apricots
½ cup water
1 glass Madeira
  Sugar to taste

Stone the apricots and remove the kernels from the stones. Pound them in a mortar and put into a saucepan with the fruit and water. Simmer until soft. Add the Madeira and sugar and cook until a syrup. Put through a sieve and serve hot.

Blueberry Sauce

A traditional American sauce, this is served with waffles and pancakes in the summertime when blueberries are plentiful.

1½ cups blueberries
¼ cup sugar
  Freshly grated nutmeg
½ teaspoon freshly grated lemon peel

Put everything into a small, heavy-bottomed saucepan and simmer gently, covered, for about 5 minutes. Serve hot or cold.

Raspberry Sauce

Use fresh raspberries or raspberry jam. If you are using fresh fruit, combine equal quantities of water and brown sugar in a saucepan. Simmer until a fine syrup. Add the raspberries and simmer until you have a thick, syrupy sauce. Flavor with a liqueur such as framboise or kirsch.

If you are making the sauce with jam, heat up and add liqueur and a little water if necessary to make a thinner sauce.

Strawberry Sauce

Make as above, using strawberries.

Stuffings and Garnishes

Delicious fruit and nut garnishes decorate a table and add flavor and variety to a meal. A purée of chestnuts, fried apple slices, spiced prunes, or grilled orange slices go well with roasts, spicy stews or curries, or in buffet spreads.

Roasted nuts (page 39) can be chopped and sprinkled over meat or vegetables. Sesame seeds can be roasted in the oven and sprinkled on many meat and vegetable dishes, and they are delicious in salads. Grated lemon rind or orange rind are good in sauces.

Stuffings seem to improve most roasts. Goose, turkey, and chicken are particularly good stuffed with an unusual stuffing such as apricots and cracked wheat; Brazil nuts, tangerines and wild rice; or apples and walnuts. The turkey dinner is transformed when the bird is stuffed with chestnuts and celery, garnished with spiced fruits, and served with a fruit sauce.

Chestnuts

Chestnuts go with game, pork, turkey, and duck, and with vegetables such as Brussels sprouts, cabbage, onions, and carrots. They are also used in stuffings and as garnishes for meat and vegetable dishes. They have an outside shell and a bitter inside skin that are extremely difficult to peel when the chestnut is raw. Once prepared in either of the following ways, however, the process is easy, but it takes a little time. If you cannot handle hot food, then I suggest you wear a pair of rubber gloves to peel them.

Slit the skins of the chestnuts. Roast them for 15 to 20 minutes in a preheated 350° F. oven. Take out and peel a few at a time, while hot. If allowed to cool, they will become extremely difficult to peel.

The other way to prepare them is to drop the chestnuts into boiling water for 8 minutes. Turn the heat off and peel them, taking a few out at a time so that they remain hot.

Purée de Marrons (*Chestnut Purée*)

Serve with roast meat, fowl, game, or cold meat.

1   pound chestnuts, peeled (page 135)
2   stalks celery, with leaves, chopped
    Herb bouquet (thyme, parsley, and bay leaf tied in cheesecloth)
    Stock, or half stock and half milk, half water and half milk, to cover
2   tablespoons butter
3   tablespoons cream or liquid from roast meat or fowl
    Pinch sugar if necessary
    Coarse salt and freshly ground white pepper

Simmer the chestnuts for an hour with the celery and herb bouquet in the stock. When cooked, remove the herb bouquet and purée in a blender or sieve them. Return them to the pan and stir in the butter, cream, sugar, and seasoning.

Braised Chestnuts

To accompany turkey, chicken, game, pork, etc.

1   pound chestnuts, peeled (page 135)
¾   pint veal stock or chicken
½   tablespoon arrowroot mixed with 1 tablespoon port
     Herb bouquet (thyme, parsley, and bay leaf tied in cheesecloth)
     Parsley sprigs
     A few chopped celery leaves if available
2   tablespoons butter

Put the chestnuts into a baking dish. Mix the stock with the arrowroot mixture. Pour over the chestnuts. Add the remaining ingredients and bake in a preheated 325° F. oven for 1 hour. Toss in the butter and serve.

Deviled Chestnuts

Good with ham, bacon, or cold turkey.

Cook the chestnuts as for Chestnut Purée (above), without puréeing them, of course. Remove them from the stock with a perforated spoon, reserving the stock for use in another dish. Season with coarse salt and cayenne pepper.

Heat a little olive oil or bacon fat in a frying pan and fry the chestnuts gently for a few minutes without breaking them. Serve hot.

Spiced Crab Apples

Serve these with turkey, goose, or game.

1	pint white vinegar
2¼	cups sugar
1	cinnamon stick
6	cloves
2	pounds crab apples, with stems on

Bring the vinegar, sugar, cinnamon stick, and cloves to boil. Reduce heat, add apples, and cook until the apples are tender. Do not overcook or stir the apples or you will get crab apple sauce. Leave the apples to cool overnight in the syrup.

If the syrup seems too thin, drain off and boil to reduce. Put the apples into jars, pour on the syrup, and seal tightly.

Spiced Apricots

These are good with goose, turkey, chicken, pork, and game.

½	cup water
1	cup white wine
2	tablespoons vinegar
5	peppercorns
2	cloves
1	stick cinnamon
3	tablespoons brown or white sugar
¾	pound apricots

Bring the water and wine to boil with the remaining ingredients except the apricots. Add the washed apricots and simmer until tender (about 15 minutes). Remove with a slotted spoon. Reduce the syrup over high heat, pour onto the apricots, and serve cold.

Spiced Prunes

Serve with goose, poultry, beef, pork, and ham.

2	pounds prunes
	Cinnamon stick, 4 whole allspice, and 4 cloves tied in cheesecloth
3	cups water
1	cup vinegar
1½	cups brown sugar

Combine all ingredients in a large saucepan and simmer for about 45 minutes or until the prunes are tender. Remove cheesecloth. Put in clean jars and seal tightly. Keep in a cool place.

Baked Apples with Raisins

Go with grilled ham, chicken, duck, or pork.

6 cooking apples
3 tablespoons soft butter
3 tablespoons sugar
2 tablespoons raisins
  Calvados (apple brandy), or regular brandy if Calvados is not available

Core apples but do not peel. Fill the cavities with a mixture of the soft butter, sugar, and raisins, which have been soaked in the Calvados. Either place in a greased baking dish and bake for about 30 minutes in a preheated 325° F. oven or wrap each one separately in foil and bake over hot coals until tender.

Baked Apples Paysanne

6 cooking apples
3 tablespoons soft butter
3 tablespoons brown sugar
  Cinnamon
1 teaspoon grated lemon rind

Core apples but do not peel. Fill the cavities with a mixture of the soft butter, brown sugar, dash of cinnamon, and lemon rind. Cook as above and serve hot with pork or chilled with cold meat.

Spiced Apples

Serve with ham, pork, or goose.

4 large cooking apples
  Calvados (apple brandy) or white wine
4 whole cloves
  Cinnamon
2 bay leaves

138

Cut cored apples into slices ¼ inch thick. Put them in a shallow greased baking dish, with Calvados or white wine to cover, with cloves, dash of cinnamon, and bay leaves. Marinate for half an hour and cook uncovered for 30 minutes.

Fried Apple Slices

4 apples
   Butter or bacon fat

Core and slice apples ¼ inch thick without peeling them. Fry them gently in butter or bacon fat, turning once, and serve them with sausages, bacon, pork, or ham.

Grilled Orange Slices

Serve these very hot with veal, ham, pork, or duck. Slice orange, peeled, an inch thick and dip in melted butter. Grill over hot coals or under broiler and sprinkle with brown sugar so that it will caramelize as they cook.

Grilled Pineapple Slices

Serve these very hot with pork or ham. Peel a pineapple and cut the flesh into strips about an inch wide. Dip in melted butter and proceed as above.

Grilled Bananas

These are good for outdoor cooking. For Fried Bananas see page 54. Grill the bananas in their skins, turning occasionally until they are quite black. Serve with pork, curries, or ham.

Bananas Grilled with Bacon

Serve these as hors d'oeuvres or with grilled meat. Cut the bananas in half and sprinkle with lemon juice to keep them from turning brown. Wrap a thick piece of bacon around each one and secure it with a skewer. Grill until the bacon is cooked.

Grilled Figs or Dates with Bacon

These are delicious with grilled pork or ham, turkey, duck, or chicken.
 Pit the dates, wrap the fruit with bacon, and secure with a toothpick. Bake over hot coals or under broiler.

Apricot and Cracked Wheat Stuffing

Good with turkey or goose.

 1 pound dried apricots
 2 cups port
 2 cups cracked wheat
 4 cups water
 4 tablespoons butter
 2 onions, chopped
 2 stalks celery, plus leaves, chopped
 Thyme, marjoram
 Coarse salt and freshly ground pepper
 4 tablespoons pine nuts
 ½ to 1 cup meat or chicken stock

 Soak the apricots in the port and the cracked wheat in the water overnight. Drain the apricots and reserve the port; drain the wheat and discard the water. Squeeze it well.
 Melt the butter in a large skillet and soften the onions with the celery and herbs. Add the wheat and cook for 5 minutes. Add the pine nuts, apricots, port left over from soaking, and ½ cup of stock. Mix thoroughly and cook for 5 more minutes. Add salt and pepper. If the stuffing seems too dry, moisten with more stock. Enough for 10-pound turkey or goose.

Sausage and Chestnut Stuffing

For goose or turkey.

1½   pounds chestnuts, prepared according to page 135
2   pounds pork sausage meat
1   onion, finely chopped
2   tablespoons butter
     Turkey or goose liver, giblets, heart, and gizzard
1   stick celery, with leaves, chopped
     Dash allspice
     Dash thyme
     Coarse salt and freshly ground pepper
1   egg

Put the chestnuts into a bowl with the sausage meat. Soften the onion in the butter and add to the bowl with the remaining ingredients. Mix well, season, and stuff into cavity. For 10- or 12-pound bird.

Tangerine and Wild Rice Stuffing

Enough for one 10-pound goose or two 5- to 6-pound chickens or ducks.

4   ounces (1 stick) butter
2   onions, finely chopped
4   stalks celery, diced (with leaves)
1   green pepper, diced
3   tangerines
5   cups cooked wild rice
½   cup pulverized nuts
½   cup stock made from giblets
     Coarse salt and freshly ground pepper
½   teaspoon thyme
     Dash marjoram

Melt the butter in a skillet. Gently fry the onions with the celery and pepper until soft.

Meanwhile, peel the tangerines, remove membrane and seeds, and cut sections in half. Chop the peel of one tangerine very small and simmer for 10 minutes in water to cover. Drain.

Combine all the ingredients in a mixing bowl and stuff into cavity.

Chestnut and Apple Stuffing

For goose or turkey.

2   pounds chestnuts, prepared according to page 135
1   pound apples, peeled, quartered, and cored
6   ounces lean pork belly or salted pork
1   cup milk
2   shallots, finely chopped
2   tablespoons chopped fresh parsley
2   eggs
    Coarse salt and freshly ground black pepper

Chop the chestnuts and put into mixing bowl. Stew the apples in a little water until soft. Dice the pork and simmer 10 minutes in water to cover.

Mix all the ingredients together in a large bowl. Season and stuff into cavity. For 10- to 12-pound bird.

Walnut Stuffing

For 10-pound turkey or two 5- to 6-pound chickens.

14   slices brown bread
 6   tablespoons butter
 2   onions, finely chopped
 1   garlic clove, finely chopped
 4   stalks celery, plus leaves, finely chopped
     Turkey liver, chopped
 1   cup chopped walnuts
     Coarse salt and freshly ground pepper
½   teaspoon sage
½   teaspoon thyme
 2   tablespoons chopped fresh parsley
½   cup brandy or red wine

In the blender reduce the bread, a little at a time, to bread crumbs.

Heat the butter in a skillet and gently soften the onion with the garlic and celery. Add the liver and cook for 3 minutes.

Combine all the ingredients in a mixing bowl. Stuff into bird.

Sausage and Apple Stuffing

For goose or turkey.

2 pounds pork sausage meat
6 apples, peeled, quartered, and cored
2 onions, chopped
1 cup fresh white bread crumbs
  Dash thyme
  Coarse salt and freshly ground pepper
2 eggs, lightly beaten
4 tablespoons butter

Soften the onions in the butter. Add the apples and stew until soft. Put into mixing bowl with remaining ingredients. Bind thoroughly with the egg, season, and stuff into cavity. For 10- to 12-pound bird.

Celery, Apple, and Walnut Stuffing

For goose or turkey.

2 onions, chopped
3 tablespoons butter
4 stalks celery, with leaves, chopped
2 apples, peeled, quartered and chopped
4 ounces walnut meats, chopped
  Dash thyme
2 tablespoons chopped fresh parsley
  Coarse salt and freshly ground black pepper
3 to 4 tablespoons thick cream

Soften the onions in the butter. Add the celery and apples and cook until the apples are soft.

Combine in a mixing bowl with the remaining ingredients. Bind with the cream, adding more if necessary. Season and stuff into cavity. For 10- to 12-pound bird.

Brazil Nut Stuffing

For turkey or chicken. (Use a quarter the amount for one chicken.)

14 slices brown bread
2 cups Brazil nuts
2 onions, chopped
1 stick (4 ounces) butter
½ pound mushrooms, chopped
1 cup diced celery, plus leaves
1 teaspoon thyme
½ cup stock made from giblets
  Dash sage
  Coarse salt and freshly ground pepper
  Dash cayenne pepper

In a blender reduce the bread, a little at a time, to crumbs. Pulverize the Brazil nuts in the same way.

Soften the onion in the butter. Add the mushrooms, celery, and thyme. Cook for about 5 minutes. Add the stock; cook 5 minutes more. Combine all the ingredients in the mixing bowl, season, and stuff into bird.

Chutneys, Pickles, Preserves, and Brandied Fruit

Almost every kitchen has a cool, dark, dry corner or shelf where bottles of pickles, jams, jellies, and chutneys can be stored. There are few things more satisfying to a cook than a shelf filled with these little pots of varying colors and hues. Homemade red-currant jelly is so much better with a roast than the commercial kind, brandied peaches are one of the most delicious desserts imaginable, and of course there is nothing like home-made chutneys to go with cold meat and poultry or homemade jam with slices of fresh bread.

Jams are not nearly so complicated to make as one would think. More and more people are making their own in revolt against the flat and oversweet taste of store-bought jams. You don't need a farm kitchen for preparing jam. The fruit must be sound and fresh, not over- or underripe, and dry, otherwise it will not set properly. To test jam, put a teaspoonful of cooked jam on a plate and cool. When you tilt the plate a skin will form over it, and it will set into a jelly if it is done.

Use Mason-type jars or jelly jars to store the jam. They should be thoroughly washed and placed—lids, rubber rings, and all—in water and boiled for 5 minutes. Just before you are ready to use them, turn them upside down on a rack to dry. Fill the pots to within ¼ inch of the top. Fill the remaining space with ⅛ inch paraffin. Let cool until it sets; then put another ⅛ inch on top. To prepare paraffin, shave the bar into the top of a double boiler and melt over hot water. When you are ready to seal the pots, wipe off any jam from the rim and pour the paraffin in, swirling it around so that the jam is completely covered. Let it set; then repeat. Alternatively, a piece of paper dipped in brandy will help preserve the jam. Put the name and date of the jam on the jar and store in a dark place.

Chutneys and pickles are even simpler to make than jams and jellies, and they are a vast improvement over the often harsh and overseasoned commercial chutneys. They should be packed into jars that can be sealed with a rubber ring. Brandied fruits should also be stored this way.

Brandied Cherries

6   pounds large red or white cherries
¼   cup granulated sugar (per jar)
    Brandy

Wash and drain about 6 pounds large red or white ripe cherries, discarding any bad ones. Cut the stems to ½ inch.

Pack the cherries into quart glasses or jars, adding about ¼ cup granulated sugar to each jar and alternating layers of cherries and sugar. When ¾ full, fill to the brim with brandy. Turn upside down and reverse.

Keep the jars in a cool, dry place and shake gently each week for a month. Store for 2 months before using.

If you are using pint jars, halve the amount of sugar you put into each jar.

Brandied Peaches

8   pounds fresh peaches
5   pounds sugar
5   cups water
4   vanilla beans (optional)

Scald 8 pounds fresh peaches, a few at a time, in boiling water and remove the skins.

Boil 5 pounds sugar in 5 cups water until the sugar is dissolved. Drop in the peaches and simmer until tender. Remove with a slotted spoon to four 1-quart sterilized jars.

Boil the syrup until thick and reduced by a third. Pour over the peaches in the jars until about ⅔ full. If you like, put a 1½-inch vanilla bean in each jar.

Seal and put in a cool, dry place. Shake once a day for a week. Let stand for a month before you use them. They will keep for several years.

146

Blueberry Jam

8 cups blueberries
2 cups white sugar
2 cups brown sugar
  Juice of 1 lemon
1 teaspoon powdered cinnamon
¼ teaspoon nutmeg

Crush the blueberries slightly in a large china bowl and mix with the sugar, lemon juice, and spices. Let the mixture stand overnight. Bring to boil over high heat and simmer for about 15 minutes until thick. Put in sterilized jars and seal with ⅛ inch paraffin wax.

Blackberry and Orange Jam

6 cups blackberries
½ cup water
¾ cup orange juice
  Juice of 1 lemon
1 tablespoon grated orange peel
7 cups sugar

Cook the blackberries in the water until they are heated through. Sieve half of them and return the purée to the saucepan. Add the remaining ingredients and bring to full boil, stirring constantly. Simmer until thick and remove from heat. Stir for several more minutes so that the berries won't rise to the top. Pour into sterilized jars and seal with ⅛ inch paraffin wax.

Peach Jam

4 pounds peaches
  About 4 pounds sugar
1 cup water

Drop the peaches into boiling water for 1 minute and drain. Slip off their skins, cut them in half, and remove their stones.

Weigh them and combine in a saucepan with an equal amount of sugar and the water. Cook until transparent, pour into sterilized jars, and seal with ⅛ inch paraffin wax.

Rhubarb and Ginger Jam

6   pounds rhubarb, chopped
6   pounds sugar
6   lemons, thinly sliced
½   cup chopped preserved ginger

Combine the rhubarb with the sugar and lemon. Let the mixture stand overnight in a china bowl. Next day add ginger, bring to boil, and simmer for about 45 minutes. Do not stir too much. The pieces of rhubarb should remain whole. Pour into sterilized jars and seal with ⅛ inch paraffin wax.

Grapefruit Marmalade

3   large grapefruit
2½ to 3   quarts cold water
8 to 10   cups sugar

Peel the grapefruit very thin without cutting into the white pith. Cut the peel into *julienne* (fine strips about 1 inch long and ⅛ inch wide). Cut away the white peel and discard. Halve or quarter the pulp and put it into a damp cheesecloth. Bring up the ends, tie securely, and squeeze out the juice into a large bowl. Add enough water to make 3 quarts. Drop in the peel and the bag of pulp. Let the mixture stand overnight.

In a large kettle bring the mixture to boil and simmer uncovered over low heat for 2 hours. Discard cheesecloth and pulp and measure the mixture. Add 1 cup sugar to each cup liquid. Cook over moderate heat, stirring until the sugar is dissolved. Increase the heat and bring to boil for 30 minutes or until thermometer registers 220° F.

Skim off foam. Put the marmalade into hot sterilized jars or jelly glasses and seal with paraffin wax.

Cranberry Preserve with Brazil Nuts

4   cups cranberries
1   cup water
1½   cups white sugar
1   cup brown sugar
1   cup seedless raisins
½   cup orange juice
⅓   cup grated lemon rind
1   cup chopped Brazil nuts (unsalted)

Simmer the cranberries in the water until they are soft. Put through sieve or food mill and discard seeds and skin. Combine them in a saucepan with the remaining ingredients and simmer for about 15 minutes. Cool and store in tightly sealed jars.

Guava Paste

Cut the tops off some guavas and rub the fruit through a sieve. Weigh the pulp and combine it in a saucepan with the same weight of sugar. Simmer over medium heat until the mixture becomes stiff and starts to shrink from the sides of the pan. Put into a greased, sugared tin and cool. When cool, sprinkle with icing sugar and cut into squares. Store in a cool place.

Plum Jam

To each pound of red or blue plums use the same weight of sugar. Wash the plums, cut them in half, and remove the stones. Combine them with the sugar and leave for a couple of hours. Put into a saucepan and stir over low heat to dissolve the sugar. Bring to boil and simmer until thick. Skim off the foam, put in jars, and seal with ⅛ inch paraffin wax.

Gooseberry Jam

For each pound of topped and tailed gooseberries you need ¼ cup water and ¾ pound sugar. Simmer the fruit in the water for 15 minutes. Add the sugar and dissolve over low heat. Boil briskly, stirring, for about 20 minutes. Pour into jars and seal with ⅛ inch paraffin wax.

Apricot and Date Chutney

This is good with tongue or ham.

1	pound dried apricots
1½	cups sultanas or raisins
1½	cups vinegar
1	cup water
1½	cups brown sugar
½	cup chopped ginger
1½	tablespoons salt
1	teaspoon ground coriander seeds

Combine all ingredients in a large saucepan and simmer for 2 hours over low heat. Cool, pour into jars, and seal.

Pineapple Chutney

1	large pineapple
1	teaspoon coarse salt
1	clove garlic
1	cup sugar
1	cup vinegar
1	cinnamon stick
1	teaspoon chopped dried chilis
¼	teaspoon ground cloves
2	cups seedless raisins or sultanas

Peel and chop the pineapple. Salt it and let it stand for 2 hours. Chop the garlic. Combine the sugar, vinegar, and spices in a saucepan and bring to boil. Add the pineapple and raisins and cook over medium heat until thick (about 1 hour). Put into jars and seal.

Apple Chutney

This chutney improves if it is cooked very slowly for a long time. If you can, you should let it simmer very gently on the back of the stove all day. Otherwise, 3 hours will do.

  3   pounds apples, peeled, cored, and chopped
  1   pound onions, chopped
  2   cups seedless raisins or sultanas
  2   cups brown sugar
1½   cups vinegar
  1   tablespoon mustard seed, crushed
  2   ounces fresh ginger, chopped
  1   teaspoon cayenne pepper
  1   tablespoon crushed coriander seeds
  1   clove garlic, finely chopped (optional)
  1   tablespoon pulverized dried chili

Combine all the ingredients and simmer over low heat. Stir frequently as the mixture begins to thicken toward the end. Cool and put into sterilized jars and seal. Keep in a cool place.

Mango Chutney

Ripe or green mangoes can be used.

  8   mangoes
  1   cup vinegar
  1   stick cinnamon
  ½   teaspoon allspice
  ½   teaspoon ground cloves
  ½   teaspoon ginger or 1 tablespoon chopped fresh
  2   cups raisins
  1   cup brown sugar
  1   cup water

Peel and remove the stones from the mangoes; cut them up. Combine the vinegar and spices and bring to boil. Add the mangoes and raisins, sugar and water, and simmer for about 30 minutes. Cool, pour into hot sterile jars, and store in a cool place.

Desserts

There are enough delicious fruit desserts to write a book about them alone. After a heavy meal there are few things more rewarding than fresh fruit and cheese or a light fruit dessert. Heavy pastries and complicated desserts are out of place, and in any case it is much easier to buy them than to make them yourself. Simple rather than elaborate fruit desserts make up this chapter, with one or two greedy exceptions that have been put in because I cannot resist them.

In America cooked fruit is often preferable to fresh fruit because the latter is so often not fresh and frequently rather tasteless, having been artificially grown with chemicals and picked when unripe.

When liqueurs are mixed with fruits, only the smaller amounts should be used, otherwise they will overwhelm the delicate flavor. When you are flaming desserts, heat the liqueur first, or it may not catch on fire.

Fruit Compôte

Next to fresh fruit, fruit compôtes are one of the best desserts. They are extremely easy to make but very often seem to go wrong. The fruit should not be cooked to a mush; it should look fresh when it has been cooked. Too much water, overcooking, and sugar added at the end instead of the beginning are often the reasons why the compôte is a failure.

The syrup must be made first. Allow about ¼ pound of sugar to each pound of fruit, depending on the sweetness of the fruit. Put it into a saucepan with 1 cup water and simmer for 5 to 10 minutes. *Then* add the fruit. Poach it, and when it is done, remove it with a slotted spoon. Boil the syrup to reduce it, and when thick, pour it over the fruit in a serving dish. Chill before serving.

Flavorings such as vanilla, mace, ginger, cloves, cardamom, cinnamon, coriander, and nutmeg can be added to the syrup before it is cooked. Lemon peel can also be added. Elder flowers are marvelous with gooseberries. The syrup can also be flavored with brandy, kirsch, rum, and fruit liqueurs.

If you are making a mixed fruit compôte, poach the fruits separately. Combine the syrups and reduce. Then pour the syrup over the mixed fruit.

Some good combinations are:
    apples and tangerines
    apples and blackberries
    nectarines and raspberries
    apricots and strawberries
    apricots, peaches, and plums
    blueberries and peaches
    strawberries and rhubarb
    pineapple and raspberries
    bananas and pears

Fruit Mousse

A light fruit mousse is a very good summer dessert. Make a purée by poaching the fruit as for Fruit Compôte (opposite) but either cooking the fruit until it is a purée or puréeing in the blender or through a sieve.

As for flavoring, try vanilla or lemon with apple mousse, lemon with raspberry, orange with rhubarb, almond with cherry, white or red wine with strawberry, sherry with red currant.

    1   cup fruit purée
    1   ounce castor sugar
    ½   ounce gelatin
    2   tablespoons water or fruit juice
    1   cup heavy cream
  2 to 3   egg whites

Combine the purée and sugar in a bowl and add whatever flavorings you choose. Melt the gelatin in the water and stir into the purée. Whip the cream. Whip the egg whites until they stand in peaks. Fold the cream and whites into the purée. Pour into a dish and chill.

Serves 2–3.

153

Crêpes

After a light meal, crêpes make a delicious dessert. They don't have to come flaming to the table in a grandiose manner. You can fill them with all kinds of different fruits, poached or puréed, or fruit sauces and preserves. They are simple to make and will keep in the refrigerator, although they will not be so good as they are when freshly made.

    3   eggs
    1   cup milk
    6   tablespoons flour
        Pinch salt
    2   tablespoons melted butter
    2   tablespoons liqueur (kirsch, Cointreau, etc.)

Combine all the ingredients in a blender and mix until smooth. Scrape any flour that sticks to the sides with a spatula and blend in. Leave for 1 to 2 hours before using. Makes about 12 crêpes.

To cook crêpes, use a frying pan about 8 inches across. Heat the pan and wipe it around with a paper towel dipped in a little oil. When the pan begins to smoke, spoon in about 1 tablespoon of batter and tilt the pan so that it spreads over the bottom in a thin layer. Pour off any excess batter. When it starts to curl, lift the pancake with a fork, or, better still, with your fingers. Turn it over quickly and cook it for a couple of minutes. Remove it to a plate and keep warm. Your crêpe is now ready for stuffing.

Clafouti

A rich French dessert. You need black cherries to get the best results, but blackberries or raspberries will do as a substitute.

    3   eggs
    1   cup flour
    ⅓   cup sugar
    1   cup milk, boiling
    2   cups stoned black cherries
        Powdered sugar

Stir the eggs one at a time into the flour. Add the sugar and boiling milk and mix thoroughly, taking out all the lumps. Let stand for 2 hours.

Pour the batter into a buttered baking dish. Cover with the cherries and bake for 35 minutes in a preheated 325° F. oven. Sprinkle with sugar and serve.

Marmelade de Pommes

1½ pounds apples
    Grated lemon peel
 2 tablespoons sugar
 2 ounces butter

Peel, core, and chop the apples. Cook over very low heat, stirring occasionally, with the lemon peel and the sugar. When soft, whip in the butter. You should have a thick purée.

Serve with cream, hot or cold.

Apple Charlotte

The trick is to line the mold tightly so that the applesauce does not escape.

Stale bread
Melted butter
Double quantity Marmelade de Pommes (see above)
Apricot Sauce, page 133

Dip slices of stale bread in melted butter and line a mold. Fill with Marmelade de Pommes and cover with bread. Cook for 30 minutes in a preheated 400° F. oven. Serve with apricot sauce.

Apple Crisp

A simple dessert without the fuss of pastry making.

 4 tablespoons porridge oats
 3 tablespoons melted butter
 2 tablespoons brown sugar
1½ pounds apples, peeled, cored, and sliced
    Cinnamon
 4 cloves
    Lemon juice
    Sugar to taste

Combine the oats, melted butter, and sugar. Mix and spread on a piece of foil paper. Cook for 10 minutes in a moderate oven, stirring once or twice with a fork.

Meanwhile, gently cook the apples with the remaining ingredients in a saucepan. Put into a greased baking dish and top with the oats. Bake in a moderate oven for 20 to 30 minutes.

Baked Apricots

If you like, sour or fresh cream can be served with the apricots.

2 pounds apricots
2 tablespoons sugar
1 piece vanilla bean
  Dash kirsch (optional)

With the point of a knife slice the apricots down one side but leave whole. Put into a baking dish, sprinkle with sugar, and add the vanilla essence and kirsch. Put in enough water to cover the bottom of the dish. Bake in a preheated 325° F. oven for an hour.

Serves 4.

Note: Sugar that has been stored with a vanilla pod is just as good. If you have some, I suggest you use it instead.

Baked Bananas

A cheap and rewarding dish. Serve it with heavy cream, if you like.

4 bananas
  Juice of 1 lemon
  Brown sugar
3 tablespoons butter
¼ cup rum

Peel the bananas, cut them in half, and put them in a buttered baking dish. Squeeze on the lemon juice, sprinkle with brown sugar, and dot with butter. Bake in a preheated 350° F. oven for 15 to 20 minutes. Heat the rum, pour it over the bananas, and set it alight.

Serves 4.

Blackberries with Macaroons

Other fresh berries such as strawberries, raspberries, or blueberries may be substituted for blackberries.

12 to 16 fresh almond macaroons
  ½ cup rum, kirsch, or orange liqueur
  2 cups vanilla ice cream
  3 cups fresh blackberries
  1 cup whipped cream
  1 teaspoon sugar
  1 teaspoon liqueur
  1 tablespoon chopped almonds

Put the macaroons in a large glass or china dish. Pour on the rum and leave overnight. When ready to serve, spread on the ice cream, then the blackberries, and pipe the whipped cream flavored with sugar and liqueur around it. Decorate with chopped almonds and serve.
Serves 4.

Blueberries with Chestnut Purée

1 17-ounce can of chestnut purée (*crème de marrons*)
1 pound blueberries
½ pint heavy cream
  Dash of kirsch

Arrange the purée in the center of a serving dish. Put the blueberries around it, sprinkling them with a little aromatic bitters if you like.

Whip the cream and add a little kirsch for flavor. You don't need any sugar; the *marrons* are sweet enough. Pipe the cream around the *marrons* and serve.
Enough for 4.

Figs with Honey

You can use slightly overripe figs for this dish.

16 figs
¼ cup clear honey
½ cup boiling water
¼ pint heavy cream
  Dash kirsch

Cut the figs into quarters. Put the honey into a large bowl and add the water. Stir well to thin out the honey; add the figs and coat with the syrup. Chill overnight. Serve with cream flavored with a little kirsch.
Serves 3 to 4.

Figs with Kirsch

Select 12 ripe figs and prick all over with a fork. Cover with kirsch and leave overnight. Set alight before serving to remove the harsh taste of the alcohol.
Serves 3 to 4.

Gooseberry Fool

2   pints gooseberries
½   cup water
½   cup sugar
¼   pint heavy cream

Top and tail the gooseberries and cook in the water with the sugar until tender. Put through a sieve and add more sugar to taste. Whip the cream and fold it in. Chill and serve.

Grapes with Sour Cream

Choose seedless grapes. Put them into a serving bowl and coat them with sour cream. Sprinkle on plenty of thick dark brown sugar and serve.
Note: Bananas may also be served this way.

Guayabas con Queso (Guavas with Cream Cheese)

This dessert can be found in almost every Latin American restaurant. It is one of the simplest. Often it is served with salted crackers, but I find these unnecessary.
You need a can of guava shells and a package of cream cheese. For each person allow 2 or 3 guava shells and serve them on a plate with a chunk of cream cheese.

Cold Lemon Soufflé

5   eggs
½   cup sugar
    Juice and grated rind of 2 lemons
½   ounce gelatin
¼   cup cold water

Beat the yolks with the sugar until lemon-colored. Add the lemon juice
and rind and whisk in the top of a double boiler until thick. Add the
gelatin dissolved in cold water. Cool and fold in stiffly beaten egg whites.
Chill until set. Serve with cream if you like.
Serves 4.

Fresh Lichee Nuts

Since these are not often available, you may have to use canned ones.
Use them with their juice and serve them chilled.

If you are using fresh nuts, peel off the tough outer skin. Put them into
a bowl with a little kirsch, a dash of sugar, and a little fresh mint chopped
on top. Chill until ready to serve.

Tropical Fruit Salad

This salad is for people lucky enough to be within reach of these fresh
fruits. Peel and slice the flesh of a ripe pineapple, papaya, and 3 or 4
mangoes and peel some lichee nuts. Put them into a bowl with a little
lemon or lime juice, sugar (not much), and some kirsch or other suitable
liqueur. Serve chilled.

Mangoes with Papaya Sauce

    About 4 to 6 ripe mangoes
    Vanilla ice cream
2   cups ripe papaya pulp
    Juice of 1 lime
    Rum
    Chopped almonds to garnish

Line 4 glasses with peeled, pitted, chopped mangoes. Put a dollop of vanilla ice cream on top. Reduce the papaya pulp to a purée in the blender with the lime juice. Flavor with rum, pour onto the ice cream, and top with almonds.

Serves 4.

Mixed Melon Dessert

Scoop out the insides of a watermelon, cantaloupe, and honeydew. Use a scooper that will make round balls if you have one; otherwise chop the melon into 1-inch squares. Sprinkle with lemon and ginger. If you are serving this at a party, you can use the melon skin as a receptacle for the fruit.

Serves 12 to 14.

Pineapple Stuffed with Fruit

Cut the inside from a large ripe pineapple without breaking the skin. You can do this by slicing off the top and scooping out the flesh from the inside. Fill the pineapple shell with strawberries, raspberries, chopped bananas sprinkled with lemon juice, and diced pineapple. A little fruit liqueur or kirsch is excellent.

Watermelon Stuffed with Fruit

This is a simple and excellent dessert for a summer party. Vary the amount of the fruit you use as you please. Light sugar cookies go well with this dessert.

Half a watermelon, flesh scooped out
1   small honeydew melon
1   pineapple
2   quarts strawberries
1   pound apricots
1   pound peaches
    Powdered sugar
    Juice of 3 limes
    About ½ cup kirsch

If you have a fruit scooper that will make the melons into little balls, use it. Otherwise chop the melons into small, even squares. Leave the skin of the watermelon intact. Peel and chop the pineapple. Leave the strawberries whole unless they are abnormally large. Slice the apricots and peaches. You can peel them if you like. Do this by dropping them into boiling water so that the skins slip off easily.

Arrange the fruit in the watermelon skin. Sprinkle with sugar, lime juice, and kirsch. Refrigerate until ready to serve.

Serves 12 to 14.

Nectarines with Raspberries and Pistachios

Slice about 8 ripe nectarines into a dish. Sprinkle with sugar and arrange 1 pint raspberries over the top. Pour on some whipped cream lightly flavored with kirsch and top with pistachio nuts.

Serves 4.

Iced Persimmon

This is a cooling and refreshing summer dessert. Cut a hole in each persimmon around the stalk and scoop out the pulp without breaking the skin. Marinate the pulp in kirsch or some other liqueur and refrigerate.

Just before serving, mix the pulp with vanilla ice cream or chopped iced pineapple (or both) and fill the persimmons with the mixture.

Serves 4.

Orange in Red Wine

    6 oranges
    1 cup dry red wine
    1 cup water
 ¾ to 1 cup sugar, depending on sweetness of oranges
    4 cloves
       Dash freshly grated nutmeg
       Cinnamon stick
    ½ lemon, sliced

161

Peel the skin from three of the oranges with a vegetable peeler and reserve. Then cut away the fibrous membrane and slice the oranges. Put them into a dish.

Mix together the remaining ingredients in a saucepan and simmer for about 10 minutes. Strain onto the oranges. Meanwhile, chop the orange skins *julienne*, scatter over the slices, and chill overnight.

Enough for 6.

Baked Peaches

This is an excellent way to use the cheap, often not very ripe peaches that come on sale during the summer. The brandy is optional but makes the dish. (You can buy a miniature if you don't want to spend the money for a whole bottle.)

        6   fresh peaches
        2   tablespoons butter
        2   tablespoons sugar
      ½   cup brandy
          Heavy cream

Peel the peaches by dropping them into boiling water and removing their skins while they are still warm. Cut them in half and remove the stones.

Butter a baking dish and arrange the halves face down, overlapping, in the dish and sprinkle with sugar. Bake in a preheated 375° F. oven until tender (about 20 to 30 minutes). When ready to serve, heat the brandy in a small saucepan, pour it on the peaches, light it, and take them flaming to the table. Serve with heavy cream.

Enough for 6.

Prunes in Wine

Choose the best prunes available and put them in screw-top glass jars. Fill them to the brim with sweet red or white wine. I don't advise a sweet domestic wine; a German, Yugoslavian, Italian, or French wine would be better for this. Domestic sweet wines on the whole are rather undrinkable and those that aren't are expensive.

Leave the prunes in the wine for a month or more. Then eat them either straight from the jar or as a dessert with plenty of thick cream.

Poires au Vin Rouge

Cooked this way, the pears come out dark red in a delicious thick syrup.

6	pears
½	bottle red wine (Beaujolais, Burgundy)
	Cinnamon stick
½	cup sugar
3	tablespoons grated orange peel

Peel, halve, and core the pears. Bring the wine, cinnamon stick, sugar, and orange to the boil. Add the pears and simmer until very tender over low heat (about 1½ hours). Cool and remove cinnamon stick before serving.
Serves 6.

Glazed Pears

6	pears
1	cup sugar
2	cups water
1	vanilla bean
½	pint cream
	Kirsch

Peel, halve, and core the pears. Bring the sugar, water, and vanilla bean to boil. Add the pears and simmer until tender. Cool. Serve with whipped cream flavored with kirsch or *poire* eau-de-vie.
Serves 6.

Fried Pineapple

This is a most delicious dessert and is especially liked by those who don't enjoy pineapple raw.

Peel and slice a pineapple. Melt some butter in a frying pan and fry the slices until they are light brown on each side. Meanwhile, warm a small glass of brandy. Transfer the pineapple to a serving dish, sprinkle with sugar, pour on the brandy, and set it alight. Serve immediately.
Serves 4.

Baked Quinces

When fresh quinces are available, this makes a delicious and simple dessert.

6 quinces
1 cup sugar
1 orange, peeled and sliced
2 tablespoons orange liqueur
½ cup water
Butter

Peel, core, and slice the quinces. Place in a buttered baking dish with the remaining ingredients. Bake in a preheated 300° F. oven for 2 hours. Serves 4.

Raspberries and Cream

Raspberries are so delicate that they are really at their best served with thick cream, a little sugar, and perhaps a touch of raspberry liqueur or Madeira. If you use straight kirsch or framboise, heat it first and boil off the harsh alcohol taste that tends to overpower the raspberries. Or you can simply flavor the cream with a little liqueur.

Raspberries with Zabaglione

Pour this Italian sauce over raspberries in individual glasses. It must, of course, be made right at the last minute.

6 egg yolks
3 tablespoons sugar
⅔ cup Marsala
2 pints raspberries

Heat the egg yolks in the top of a double boiler with the sugar until thick and creamy. Add the Marsala and beat with a whisk until creamy and tripled in size. Pour over the raspberries and serve. Serves 4.

Stewed Rhubarb

The best way to stew rhubarb is in a slow oven, uncovered, so that the pieces will remain whole. Don't add any liquid. A little butter, brown sugar, or honey and some spices such as a few cloves, ground coriander, or cardamom seeds will add flavor. You can also put in a few mint leaves and lemon or orange peel. Serve it hot or cold with heavy cream or yogurt.

Rhubarb pie can be made by putting the rhubarb into a baking dish and placing a pie crust on the top. By the time the pastry is cooked, the rhubarb will be cooked, too. Don't use too hot an oven.

Crêpes with Walnut Filling and Chocolate Sauce

About 12 crêpes (page 154)

Walnut Filling
- 1½ cups ground walnuts
- 3 tablespoons sugar
- Dash bitters (optional)
- ¾ cup milk
- 1 tablespoon rum or fruit liqueur

Chocolate Sauce
- 6 squares semisweet chocolate
- 1 to 2 tablespoons sugar
- ½ cup water
- 1 egg yolk
- ¼ cup milk
- Dash rum or fruit liqueur (orange, preferably)

While you are cooking the pancakes according to the master recipe, combine the walnuts, sugar, bitters, and milk in a small saucepan. Bring to boil, stirring occasionally, and simmer for 2 minutes. Remove and stir in rum.

In the top of a double boiler melt the chocolate with the sugar and water. Mix the egg yolk with the milk and add with the liqueur. If at any time the sauce starts to dry up, add more water and mix well with a whisk.

Stuff the walnut mixture into the crêpes and arrange on a baking dish, keeping them warm in the oven. When ready to serve, pour on the chocolate sauce.

165

Strawberries Romanoff

2 pints strawberries
Juice of 2 to 3 oranges
1 tablespoon orange liqueur
1 pint heavy cream
2 tablespoons sugar

Put the strawberries in a bowl with the orange juice and orange liqueur. Refrigerate for 2 hours. Whip the cream with sugar and additional orange liqueur to taste. Pour over the strawberries and serve.

Serves 6.

Strawberries in Marsala

An Italian dessert. Red wine will do if you can't get Marsala. Combine fresh strawberries, sugar to taste, and Marsala and leave to macerate for a few hours. Serve chilled.

Index